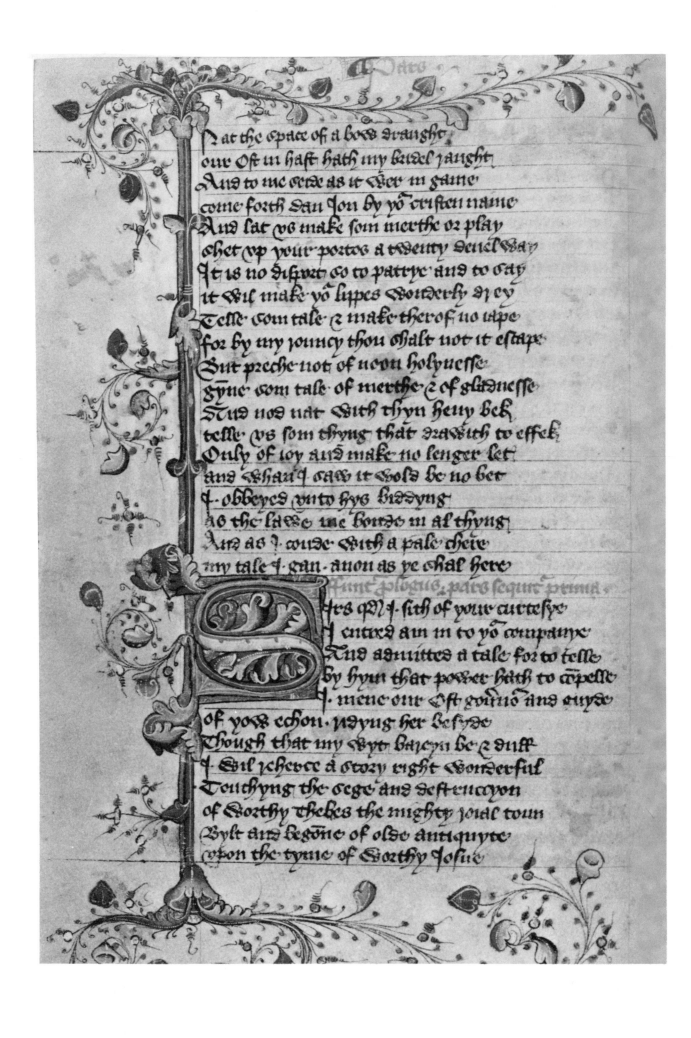

at the space of a book draught
Our Ost in haft hath my bridel caught
And to me seide as it were in game
come forth dan Jon by yo cristen name
And lat vs make som merthe or play
chet vp your portos a twenty deuel way
It is no disport co to pattye and to say
it wil make yo lippes wonderly drey
Tessell som tale & make therof no tape
for by my journey thou shalt not it escape
But preche not of noon holynesse
gyue som tale of merthe & of gladnesse
And nod nat with thyn heuy bek
telle vs som thyng that drawith to effek
Only of joy and make no lenger let
and whan I saw it wold be no bet
I obbeyed vnto hys biddyng
As the lawe me bounde in al thyng
And as I coude with a pale chere
my tale I gan anon as ye shal here

rs on I sith of your curtesye
I entred am in to yo companye
And admittes a tale for to telle
by hym that power hath to compelle
I mene our Ost gouno and guyde
of you echon, preyng her besyde
Though that my wyt barayn be & dull
I wil reherce a story right wonderful
Touchyng the sege and destruccyon
of worthy Thebes the mighty royal toun
Bylt and begone of olde antiquyte
vpon the tyme of worthy Josue

W. Bruce Finnie
University of Delaware

The Stages of English

Texts,

Transcriptions,

Exercises

HOUGHTON MIFFLIN COMPANY • BOSTON

New York • Atlanta • Geneva, Ill. • Dallas • Palo Alto

Printed in the U.S.A.
Library of Congress Catalog Card Number: 71-172123
ISBN: 0-395-12622-3

The manuscript page on the cover and frontispiece is from a copy (c. 1430) of *The Siege of Thebes* by John Lydgate. Courtesy of the Boston Public Library.

For
Arthur R. Dunlap

TABLE OF CONTENTS

ILLUSTRATIONS

ABBREVIATIONS AND SYMBOLS

EME	Early Middle English
EMnE	Early Modern English
Gmc	Germanic
GVS	Great Vowel Shift
IE	Indo-European
ME	Middle English
MnE	Modern English
OE	Old English
OF	Old French
ON	Old Norse
W Gmc	West Germanic

>	becomes/develops into
<	from/is derived from
/	or
[ ]	Symbols within brackets are the symbols of the International Phonetic Alphabet, indicating sounds, not spellings.
*	a reconstructed, hypothetical, unrecorded form

PREFACE

This book grew out of my own need as a teacher of the history of the English language for accessible and reliable texts illustrating the major periods of the language. It is especially difficult to find convenient specimens of Old English, Middle English, and Early Modern English in phonetic notation, and the time and bother spent in preparing appropriate handouts for classroom use can be overwhelming.

In the past, textbooks have often encouraged teachers merely to tell the student *about* the language. Here, the student can look at a specimen text for himself and learn to pronounce the passage by studying the accompanying notation and by listening to selected passages on the accompanying phonograph record. The exercises after each selection are designed to encourage the student to examine the texts and the passages of notation in specific ways and to discover *for himself* many of the characteristics of the major stages of the language. These exercises call attention to such matters as spelling, morphology, word order, and phonology. Translations are provided for Old English and Middle English selections. The teacher may wish to use this part of the book—Part Two—for class work or for out-of-class assignments, or he may simply allow the student to use it by himself, as needed, to supplement his understanding of the development of the language.

Part One of the book is intended to give the student enough information about the sounds of English for him to be able to use Part Two effectively. For native speakers of English, it presupposes no prior knowledge of the subject. This introductory section describes for the beginning student the sounds of Modern English and those of each of the older periods of the language. It also explains how specific sounds change from one period to another. For the advanced student, it comments on important prehistorical developments in Germanic, West Germanic, and Early Old English, so that historical Old English can be the more fully understood. Thus the first section can be treated as a working textbook or reference work, or both, depending on the needs of the student and on the level of study. It is hoped that appropriate parts of both sections of the book will be useful in Chaucer classes and in Old English classes. As a history of the language text, the book may well complement one of the general textbooks on the history of the language, such as those by Baugh, Pyles, or Robertson and Cassidy.

The twenty-eight specimen texts were selected for their variety, familiarity, and intrinsic value. Thus, the Old English period is represented by easy and familiar translations from the Gospels of *Matthew* and *Luke* and by original compositions both in verse (*Beowulf*, *Deor*, the hymn in "Cædmon's Hymn"[1]) and in prose ("Alfred's Prayer" and *The Anglo-Saxon Chronicle*).

[1] The rest of the passage entitled "Cædmon's Hymn" and the passage entitled "The Conversion of Edwin" are Old English translations of a Latin work by Bede, *Historia Ecclesiastica Gentis Anglorum*.

The famous selection, "The Conversion of Edwin," demonstrates the rich possibilities for the subsequent development of English prose, even in the genre of translation.

A selection from *The Ormulum* represents Early Middle English and the earliest attempt at spelling reform. Half of the Middle English selections are from Chaucer, including the most celebrated lines in Middle English, the beginning of "The General Prologue" to *The Canterbury Tales*. The opening lines of *Troilus and Criseyde* are given, together with a selection of exquisite verse from Book V, not usually transcribed phonetically in textbooks. Chaucer's *Treatise on the Astrolabe* afforts a passage of simple prose, and *The Parson's Tale* a typical passage of didactic prose. Two selections from the *Gospels* are repeated to allow direct comparison to Old English, and, in the next section, to Early Modern English. The late alliterative tradition associated with the north is represented by the famous lines of the Northwest Midlands poem, *Sir Gawain and the Green Knight*, describing the changing seasons; these lines can also be compared to the examples of Old English alliterative poetry. The Middle English section ends with texts of three lyrics.

Prose passages from Caxton and Malory appropriately open the Early Modern English section. No phonetic transcription has been attempted for this transitional period in the history of English sounds. In addition to selections of the unique prose of the King James Bible, there is a selection from Bacon exemplifying a plain prose style and a selection from Hooker exemplifying an ornate prose style. The final texts are well-known Shakespearean selections: two sonnets and Hamlet's speech to the players.

Ideally, the selections should be photographic reproductions of the original manuscripts so the student could see as nearly as possible what the language was like as it was recorded in the various periods. However, the student would first have to study medieval handwriting practices—a fairly formidable subject. It seemed better to follow reliable modern editions of the texts, but it must be stressed that the punctuation and capitalization practices of modern editors vary. Thus, complete consistency has not been possible. I have *not* normalized the spelling, with the single exception that the *y* of the common Old English words *ys, hys, hyne*, and *hyt* has been regularized to the more usual *i*. (Only in "The Prodigal Son" and "The Laborers in the Vineyard" has this change been necessary.) Elsewhere in the Old English texts, *i* and *y* spelling distinctions are kept and the sounds transcribed as unrounded and rounded vowels respectively, whether or not actual phonetic distinctions occur. The question of whether in late Old English *y* is merely a spelling variant of *i* or a separate vowel is complex and should not concern the beginning student. The advanced student may consult Moore and Marckwardt, *Historical Outlines*, pp. 30–31, and the Old English grammars.

To help the student, I have added dots under palatalized *c*'s and *g*'s (the latter sometimes represented by ʒ) in Old English texts, dots and hooks under long close vowels and long open vowels, respectively, in Middle English texts, and, where needed, macrons over Old English and Middle English long vowels. (If a long vowel is already indicated in the spelling by a double letter, the macron is unnecessary.) Except for poetry, I have ignored line divisions in the editions, and in biblical passages I have deleted verse

numbers when given in the original. In all cases, I have paragraphed and
have numbered lines for my own purposes. I have usually deleted the few
vertical stress marks that appear in the texts, and I have often closed the
spaces between elements of a word.

It has not seemed necessary to preserve systematically the abbreviations
in Old English texts, because of the problems in phonetic transcription;
however, so that the student may have as close an idea as practical about
the appearance of Old English manuscripts, I have kept the abbreviations
in *Cædmon's Hymn* and *Deor*. In the *Anglo-Saxon Chronicle*, I have also
retained abbreviations, except that I have expanded Ʒ to *ond* in the early
passages and to *and* in the 1066 passage. (Early scribes frequently spell the
word with an *o*, while later scribes prefer *a*. The distinction is reflected in
the phonetic transcriptions, even though it may have been purely orthographic.) I have not indicated the italicized endings of words which modern
editors sometimes use to indicate that they have expanded abbreviations.

In translating Old and Middle English passages, I have striven primarily
for accuracy. Although I have sometimes inclined toward literalness, I
have tried to follow Modern English idiom. Words are added parenthetically
either to indicate that, although they are not represented in the older text,
they are necessary in the Modern English translation or to indicate that
some older words need not be used in the modern translation.

I have chosen to transcribe the sounds of English with what are usually
thought of as phonetic, not phonemic, symbols, placing the notation within
brackets instead of slant lines. For present purposes, in order for the student
to learn to pronounce Old English, he needs to know when *f* has a *v* sound,
even if the difference isn't phonemic. The instructor can go on to explain the
phonemic structure of the language at its various stages if he chooses.

Little can be known, really, about the degrees of stress for the older
periods of the language, since our writing system is not designed to represent
stress. I have not included any stress marks in the phonetic transcriptions
in this book. The assumption is that since in Old English primary stress is
usually on the first syllable, the student can easily master the few "rules"
there are (see p. 16). Stress marks would only clutter up the transcriptions.
In Middle English and Early Modern English, the assumption is that
modern stress patterns are pretty much followed (except occasionally in
verse when the meter demands otherwise), so that the student can determine
these matters for himself.

The transcription of the Early Modern English passages is based on the
work of Helge Kökeritz (*Shakespeare's Pronunciation*, New Haven, 1953),
to whom I am greatly indebted and whom the advanced student should
consult for detailed evidence. One significant departure from Kökeritz's
practice is the consistent treatment of his [ʌ] as [ʊ] in words like *up, thus,
son, much* (which in the United States are usually pronounced [ʌ] today
and are derived from ME short *ŭ* [ʊ]), and in words like *done, blood*, which
are also usually pronounced [ʌ] today and are derived from ME long close
ọ [oɪ].

Other significant departures are the treatment of Kökeritz's *s–* [š–] in
suit as [sj–]; his *–ion* [–šn̩], [–žn] as [–sjən], [–zjən]; his *–ious* [–šəs] as [–jəs];
and his *–cial* [–š]̩] as [–sjəl].

These matters are not settled, and may never be, for it is not known just when the ME sounds gave way fully to modern ones. It may well be that practice was divided in Shakespeare's London. At any rate, I have deliberately chosen the more conservative pronunciations.

Other deviations from Kökeritz occur for purposes of simplification (where simplification can reasonably be made) and consistency, and include the following: for *you* in unstressed position, I have changed K's [u] to [uː] and his [u] in *judicious* to [ʊ]. I have consistently used [ʊ] in unstressed *do* and *to*, although he has not always done so. I have consistently used [əʊ] in words like *now* and *pronounced*, whereas K sometimes uses [əu]. K's *-y* [–ɪ] > my [–ɨ] in words like *many, modesty, very* (much as in Chaucer and in MnE), except in short words like *my*, where I have kept [–ɪ] in unstressed positions. I have also changed K's [–ən] in words like *playing* to [–ɪn] and his [æː] in words like *laugh* to [æ]. His final *-ance* [–ns] has become [–nts].

Modifications of K's symbols include the following, although no significant phonetic changes are intended: K's [ẹ] > my [ɛ]. K's [əɹ] > my [ɚ] in unstressed *or, your, for, players, nature*. His [ɔːɹ] > my [ɔːr] in words like *nor*; [ɛːɹ] > [ɛːr] in words like *tear, ears*; [oːɹ] > [oːr] in words like *o're*; [aːɹ] > [aːr] in words like *part, Termagant, virtue, observance*; [ɜːɹ] > [ɝ] in words like *first, word, purpose, 'twere* (even though these words may not yet have become so similar); [ɒ] > [ɔ] in words like *on, not, torrent, honor*; and [–o] > [–oː] in words like *fellow*.

It should be emphasized that no two readings of a given passage, even by the same person, will be exactly the same; thus any transcription is a compromise and represents only one possibility. For example, the Early Modern English pronunciation of short words like *have, and, that* will vary with the amount of stress given them. With such words, I have not tried to be consistent, only believable.

ACKNOWLEDGEMENTS

In this book, as in the classroom, I rely heavily on the teachings of the late Elliott Van Kirk Dobbie. I also wish to acknowledge my indebtedness to Professors Morton W. Bloomfield, Mary A. Ferguson, and Sheila A. Houle for offering detailed comments on the manuscript, and to Professor Robert E. Thackaberry for his continued encouragement. I am also indebted to Miss Victoria Turner of Houghton Mifflin for her editorial help.

I am especially grateful to Professor Arthur R. Dunlap, who advised me often and from whose deep knowledge of the language I have benefited immeasurably during the past several years. I am indebted to the University of Delaware in a variety of ways, especially for an Instructional Improvement Grant in 1968, which helped in the development of the exercises in Part Two.

I wish to acknowledge the following textual sources: The Old English "Prodigal Son" (*Luke* 15: 11–32) is taken from *The Holy Gospels In Anglo-Saxon, Northumbrian, and Old Mercian Versions*, ed. Walter W. Skeat, Cambridge: Cambridge University Press, 1871–1887, pp. 154–158. The Old English "Lord's Prayer" (*Matthew* 6: 9–13) and "The Laborers in the Vineyard" (*Matthew* 20: 1–16) are from *The Gospel of Saint Matthew in West Saxon*, ed. James W. Bright, Boston: D. C. Heath & Co., 1904, p. 22 and pp. 91–93, respectively. "Cædmon's Hymn" and "The Conversion of Edwin" are from *The Old English Version of Bede's Ecclesiastical History of the English People*, Part I, ed. Thomas Miller, London: Published for the Early English Text Society [O.S., 95], 1890, pp. 342, 344 and pp. 134, 136, respectively. The *Beowulf* selection is from *Beowulf and the Fight at Finnsburg*, 3rd ed., ed. Fr[iedrich] Klaeber, New York: D. C. Heath & Co., 1950, pp. 1–2. *Deor* is from *Deor*, ed. Kemp Malone, New York: Appleton-Century-Crofts, 1966. [Reprinted by permission of Methuen and Co., Ltd.] Selections from *The Anglo-Saxon Chronicle* are from *Two of the Saxon Chronicles Parallel*, Vol. I, ed. Charles Plummer, Oxford: Clarendon Press, 1892–1899, pp. 54, 88–89, 91–92, 197–198. (The selections for the years 787, 895, and 901 are from the Parker MS [A], and the selection for the year 1066 is from the Laud MS [E].) "Alfred's Prayer" is from *King Alfred's Old English Version of Boethius De Consolatione Philosophiae*, ed. Walter J. Sedgefield, Oxford: Clarendon Press, 1899, p. 149.

Selections from *The Ormulum* and selected Middle English lyrics are from *A Handbook of Middle English* by Fernand Mossé, trans. James A. Walker, Baltimore: The Johns Hopkins Press, 1952, pp. 163–165 and pp. 201–202, 207–208, respectively. [Reprinted by permission of the publisher.] Selections from Chaucer are from *The Works of Geoffrey Chaucer*, 2nd ed., ed. F. N. Robinson, Boston: Houghton Mifflin Co., 1957, pp. 17–18 ("General Prologue," *Canterbury Tales*); pp. 389, 479 (*Troilus and Criseyde*); pp. 545–

546 (*A Treatise on the Astrolabe*); and p. 229 ("The Parson's Tale," *Canterbury Tales*). [Reprinted by permission of the publisher.] The Middle English "Prodigal Son" and "Lord's Prayer" are from *The Holy Bible . . . from the Latin Vulgate by John Wycliffe and his Followers*, Vol. IV, ed. Josiah Forshall and Frederic Madden, Oxford: Oxford University Press, 1850, pp. 199–201 and p. 14, respectively. (Selections are from the right-hand columns in both cases. These columns are a late revised version, usually said to be by John Purvey in the late fourteenth century.) The passage from *Sir Gawain and the Green Knight* is from *Sir Gawain and the Green Knight*, ed. J. R. R. Tolkien and E. V. Gordon, 2nd ed., revised by Norman Davis, Oxford: Oxford University Press, 1968, p. 15. [Reprinted by permission of Clarendon Press, Oxford.]

Selections from Malory are from *The Works of Sir Thomas Malory*, 2nd ed., Vol. I, ed. Eugène Vinaver, Oxford: Oxford University Press, 1967, pp. cxlv–cxlvi and 7–8. [Reprinted by permission of Clarendon Press, Oxford.] The Early Modern English "Prodigal Son" and "Lord's Prayer" are from a facsimile of the first impression of the original 1611 edition of the King James version, *The Holy Bible, Conteyning the Old Testament, and the New . . .* Imprinted at London by Robert Barker, 1611. The facsimile consulted was produced for the World Publishing Co., Cleveland, by George Rainbird Limited and is number 354 of 1500 copies, printed in Italy (n.d.), and located at the Hugh M. Morris Library, University of Delaware. The selection from *Hamlet* is from *The Norton Facsimile: The First Folio of Shakespeare*, prepared by Charlton Hinnman, New York: W. W. Norton Co., 1968, p. 774. The Shakespearean sonnets are from *A New Variorum Edition of Shakespeare* [Vol. 24]: *The Sonnets*, Vol. I, Philadelphia: J. B. Lippincott, 1944, pp. 293, 50. The selection from Bacon's "Of Discourse" is from *Francis Bacon, Essayes*, London, 1597, in *Number 17, The English Experience: Its Record in Early Printed Books, Published in Facsimile*, New York: Da Capo Press, 1968, pp. 2–3. The selection from Hooker's sermon is from *Richard Hooker, Two Sermons Upon Part of S. Judes Epistle*, Oxford, 1614, in *Number 195, The English Experience, Its Record in Early Printed Books, Published in Facsimile*, New York, Da Capo Press, 1969, pp. 31–32.

Part One

The Development
of English

ENGLISH PHONOLOGY

English sounds, as well as those of most languages, are normally made by controlling the flow of air from the lungs through the mouth and nose. No one probably needs to be reminded, in fact, that the LUNGS, VOCAL CORDS, TONGUE, TEETH, LIPS, and NOSE are used in the production of speech sounds. But it is also useful to know about several features of the mouth. The ALVEOLAR RIDGE is the hard, bony ridge out of which the upper front teeth grow. It can be felt easily with the tip of the tongue if one says *dee*. If the tip of the tongue is slowly curled backwards, then, and run back lightly along the roof of the mouth, the HARD PALATE, or, simply, the PALATE, can be felt: it is the hard, smooth, concave top of the mouth, which the middle part of the tongue is pressed against in the pronunciation of the second syllable of the word *cookie*. If the tip of the tongue is run even farther back along the roof of the mouth, almost as far as possible, it will come to the spongy SOFT PALATE, or VELUM, which the back part of the tongue (the dorsum) is pressed against in the pronunciation of the first syllable of the word *cookie*. The GLOTTIS, located in the larynx, is the space between the vocal cords.

VOCAL APPARATUS

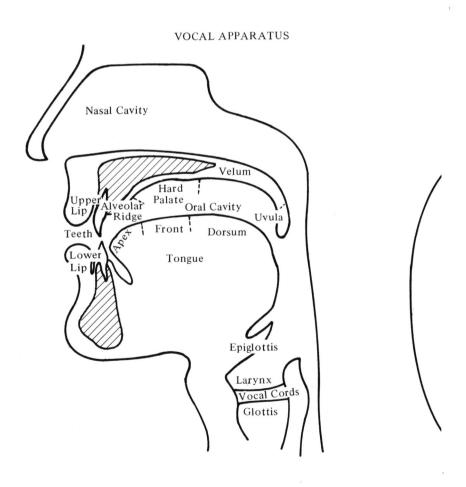

THE SOUNDS OF MODERN ENGLISH

The International Phonetic Alphabet was designed to represent the sounds of a number of modern Western languages. A modification of this system of notation will be used in this book, and, following custom, the IPA symbols and transcriptions will be placed in brackets. It must be stressed that the bracketed symbols represent *sounds*, not the names of letters.

ENGLISH CONSONANTS

The consonants of English may be either stops or continuants. A STOP is a sound which involves the complete closure of some part of the vocal apparatus during articulation. Thus the *p* and *t* sounds in *potato* [p, t] are made by blocking the air flow with the two lips for [p] and with the tongue and alveolar ridge for [t]. Similarly, the *b* and *d* sounds of *bad* [b, d] are stops, bilabial and alveolar, respectively. The other stops are the initial *k* and *g* sounds of *kill* and *gill* [k, g]. They may be either palatal, as in *kill* and *gill*, or velar, as in *cool* and *goose*; the speaker of English automatically makes the palato-velar distinction, depending on whether the adjacent vowel sound is made in the front or back of the mouth. We need not use separate IPA symbols for these variants. Sometimes a stop is accompanied by a closure of the glottis, called a GLOTTAL STOP. A glottal stop is not really a sound itself, but a method of articulation; however, it affects surrounding sounds. It may occur in what is popularly thought of as the "East Side Bowery" pronunciation of *bottle* [bɑtˀl]. In phonetic notation, it is represented by a sort of small, raised question mark without the dot beneath it. A glottal stop is often associated with a syllabic consonant (see below), and may even act as a substitute for a regular stop, as in *bottle* [bɑˀl̩].

A CONTINUANT is a sound which does not involve a complete stoppage of the air flow. It can be continuously made until one runs out of breath. All vowel sounds are continuants, and there are several kinds of consonant continuants. A FRICATIVE is a continuant made by partially restricting the flow of air so that friction is audible: the *f* and *th* sounds in *feather* [f, ð], the *th* and *v* sounds in *thieves* [θ, v], and the *h* sound in *hill* [h]. The *f* and *v* sounds are labio-dental, i.e., made by the escape of air between the lower lip and the upper front teeth, and the two *th* sounds are called apico-dental fricatives, since they are formed by placing the tip of the tongue (the apex) beneath the upper front teeth. *Then* and *thin* are a good contrasting pair of words to illustrate the [ð] and [θ] distinction. The friction of the *h* is glottal. An AFFRICATE is the combination of a stop plus a fricative, made in very quick succession, almost simultaneously. The two affricates are the apico-alveolar *ch* sounds initially and finally in *church* [č] and the apico-alveolar *j* and *dg* sounds initially and finally in *judge* [ǰ]. A NASAL is a continuant whose air flow is directed out the nose by lowering the velum to the back of the tongue. The nasals are the bilabial *m*, apico-alveolar *n*, and dorso-alveolar *–ing* sounds heard in *mining* [m, n, ŋ]. Note that for most speakers the *ing* sound [ŋ], called "eng," does not really have a final [g], although [–ŋg] is often heard in New York City. The sound [ŋ] does not occur initially in English. Sometimes the nasals, and [l] as well, are pronounced as SYLLABIC CONSONANTS. That is, if one of these sounds is unaccompanied by an audible vowel, it represents by itself a complete syllable. Examples occur in *keep 'em* (= "keep them") and in the "East Side Bowery" versions of *button* and *bottle*. In phonetic notation, a "syllabic tag" is placed under a syllabic consonant, and a glottal stop sometimes occurs immediately before the sound: [kip'm̩], [bʌt'n̩], [bɑt'l̩].

A GLIDE or SEMIVOWEL is a rapidly made continuant which occurs either immediately before or immediately after a vowel, and always in the same syllable with it. One glide is the fronto-palatal *y* sound of *yes* [j], called "jod." Note that the front part of the tongue—but not the tip—is very close to the palate and glides forward. Another glide is the apico-alveolar *r* sound of *red* [r]. Before the *r* sound is begun, there is a retroflex motion of the tongue—i.e., a backward motion of the tongue tip; this is followed by a quick forward glide of the tongue tip along the back part of the alveolar ridge. Still another glide is the *w* sound of *wet* or *wear* [w]. The lip rounding in preparation for the following vowel should be noticed. Many people, but by no means all, differentiate this *w* sound from that heard in *whet* or *where* [hw]. The fact that the *h* sound precedes the *w* sound is reflected in the OE spellings *hwettan* and *hwær*.

The apico-alveolar *l* sound, called a LATERAL, can be made in two ways. In both, the tip of the tongue is against the alveolar ridge, and the air flow is directed laterally, i.e., off the sides of the tongue. The "light" or "bright" or "clear" type of *l* [l], heard in *light*, is made in the front of the mouth after the tip of the tongue is placed against the alveolar ridge or upper teeth; the tongue tip is quickly lowered as the vowel following it is made. It frequently occurs at the beginning of a word or syllable when a front vowel immediately follows (see discussion of vowels, pp. 7 ff.). Heard in the word *dull*, the "dark" *l* sound, also [l], is formed as the tongue tip begins to assume a backward or retroflex position against the alveolar ridge. The tongue does not flick downward as it does when making the clear *l* sound. There is no reason here to use different symbols for these two sounds.

SIBILANTS include the hissing and buzzing apico-alveolar sounds of *s* and *z*, heard finally in *hiss* [s] and *buzz* [z], respectively. They also include the "hushing" fronto-palatal *sh* sound heard finally in *hush* [š]; and the French-like fronto-palatal *z* sound heard as the second element of *azure* [ž]. This last sound does not occur initially in English words.

The following is a list of Modern English consonants and their equivalents:

IPA Symbol	Description of Sound
[p]	*p* in *pill*
[b]	*b* in *bill*
[t]	*t* in *till*
[d]	*d* in *dill*
[k]	*k* in *kill*
[g]	*g* in *gill*
[f]	*f* in *fill*
[v]	*v* in *vilify*
[θ]	*th* in *thin*
[ð]	*th* in *then*
[h]	*h* in *hill*
[s]	*s* in *sill*
[z]	*z* in *zoom*

[š]	*sh* in *shrill*
[ž]	*z* in *azure*
[č]	*ch* in *chill*
[ǰ]	*j* in *Jill*, *dg(e)* in *bridge*
[r]	*r* in *rill*
[m]	*m* in *mill*
[n]	*n* in *nil*
[ŋ]	*in(g)* in *running*
[l]	*l* in *pill, light*
[w]	*w* in *wet*
[j]	*y* in *yes*

Whether a sound is VOICED or VOICELESS in English is very important. A voiced sound is one produced when the vocal cords vibrate. All vowels and diphthongs are voiced sounds, and some consonants share this characteristic. Thus, [b, d, g] are voiced, while their counterparts [p, t, k], respectively, are voiceless. In fact, this voiced–voiceless quality is the only significant difference between the two sets of sounds. By listening carefully to the distinction between the [b] in *bill* and the [p] in *pill*, for example, the student should be able to discern that the former is voiced and the latter voiceless. (If the fingers are placed on the throat over the vocal cords, vibrations can be felt when the [b] is pronounced, but not when the [p] is pronounced.) It should be carefully noted that these sounds are *not* pronounced "bee" and "pea," which are the *names* of the *letters*, not the *sounds* they *represent*. Most English sounds are voiced. In the list which follows (only the sounds we have discussed are included), notice the voiced-voiceless pairs, and notice those voiced sounds which have no voiceless counterparts:

Voiced Sounds	*Voiceless Sounds*
[b]	[p]
[d]	[t]
[g]	[k]
[v]	[f]
[ð]	[θ]
[z]	[s]
[ž]	[š]
[č]	
[ǰ]	
[r]	
[m]	
[n]	
[ŋ]	
[l]	
[w]	
[j]	
	[h]

In order to describe a sound fully, then, we should describe it as voiced or voiceless. Thus, the [k] of *kill* is a voiceless palatal stop, the [j] of *yes* is a voiced fronto-palatal glide, and so on.

ENGLISH VOWELS   The vowel chart which follows is meant to represent the open mouth as viewed from a left profile position, as on p. 3 (except with the mouth more open). The triangular chart is greatly distorted, since the mouth is more-or-less megaphone-like, the back being rather constricted, but this schematization affords the space needed to represent the points of articulation—i.e., the places in the mouth where the sounds are made. The symbols represent actual sounds, not the names of letters.

Vowel Chart

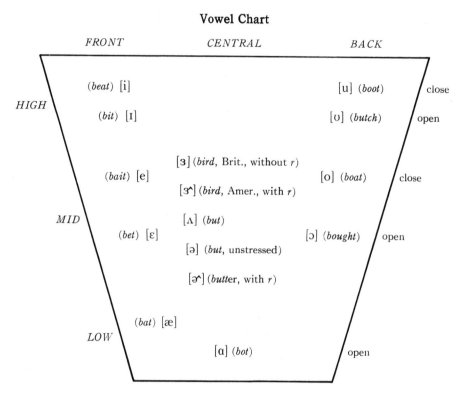

There are many other vowel sounds, of course, and those of speakers of different dialects will vary (as will those of speakers even of the same dialect sometimes), but the vowel sounds listed afford a working set for most American speakers. (New England speakers should add [a] between [ɑ] and [æ] on the chart to indicate their pronunciation of words like *aunt*.) A vowel may be referred to according to its point of articulation. The [i] of *beat* is thus a high front vowel, and the [ɔ] of *bought* a mid-back vowel. As the student makes each of the sounds, he should notice that the farther back a vowel occurs, the more open the jaws, and the farther front a vowel occurs, the less open the jaws. On the chart, the terms "open" and "close" may be thought of as referring not only to the jaw position, but also to the position of the tongue: close vowel sounds require the tongue to be relatively nearer the roof of the mouth than do corresponding open vowels; thus the tongue is held in a more tense position for close vowels. (The terms "open" and "close" are particularly useful when referring in Old English and Middle English to the two ō sounds and the two ē sounds.) Low vowels require the mouth to be open more than high vowels do, and the [ɑ] of *bot* or *father* is the most open vowel sound of all. The most frequent vowel sound of Modern English is the unstressed mid-central "schwa" sound [ə] in *but*; there is no single letter of the alphabet to represent it. The [ʌ] is virtually identical to [ə], although the mouth may be very slightly more open with [ʌ]. Convention has [ʌ] represent a stressed sound and [ə] an unstressed sound. Here, no actual phonetic distinction is intended.

ENGLISH DIPHTHONGS

A diphthong is a continuously gliding vowel sound, which begins in one position and ends in another within the same syllable. Diphthongs take relatively longer periods of time to pronounce than vowels do, and some are longer than others. If the diphthong is followed by a voiceless final consonant, less diphthongization occurs than if the diphthong is followed by a voiced consonant. The greatest diphthongization occurs when the diphthong is itself final. Note the progressively greater time of diphthongization in the sequence *height, hide, hi* or *bite, bide, by(e)*.

There are many possible diphthongs, with many variations, and the way a person pronounces them is very distinctive dialectally. Four basic diphthongs occur in Modern American English:

[aɪ]   *I, eye, style*
[aʊ]   *house, mouse*
[ɔɪ]   *boy, toy*
[ju]   *few, news*

Linguists often consider the vowel sounds in *bait* and *boat* to be diphthongs—[eɪ] and [oʊ]—but they will be treated here as the simple vowels [e] and [o]. The diphthong effect of these two sounds is less noticeable than in the other four.

THE ORIGINS OF ENGLISH

The 2000–3000 or more languages of the modern world belong to various family groups. English and most of the languages of Europe, together with some languages of Asia, belong to the Indo-European family. The theory is that prior to *c.* 3500 B.C. (±1000 years) these languages had not yet become differentiated. All of the speakers of Primitive Indo-European are believed to have lived clustered together in a fairly small geographical area (the *Urheimat*) somewhere on the Baltic coast of northern Germany between the Elbe and Vistula rivers, or perhaps somewhat to the east and south, between Lithuania and the steppes of southern Russia. About 3500 B.C., small bands of people began, for some reason, to move southward and southeasterly; later, other bands moved southwesterly and, finally, westward (see diagram below). The language of one of these last groups was Primitive Germanic, which came into existence about 800–500 B.C., and which later subdivided into three branches, West, East, and North (see diagram, p. 10). Still later, in the fifth and sixth centuries A.D., groups of West Germanic speakers, the Angles, Saxons, and Jutes, journied from modern Denmark (Jutland) and northern Germany to Britain. They came to help the native Celts defend themselves against the Picts and Scots (also Celtic), who were invading from northern and western Britain following the withdrawal of the Roman legions in 410. The Angles, Saxons, and Jutes stayed in Britain, and their culture subsumed the Celtic. The language they spoke may be called English—i.e., Old English.

Old English may be categorized into four dialects (see map, p. 19): Northumbrian, spoken in the north above the Humber River; Mercian, spoken in the central region of Britain between the Humber and the Thames; West Saxon, spoken in the south; and Old Kentish, spoken in the

THE DIFFUSION OF INDO-EUROPEAN LANGUAGES

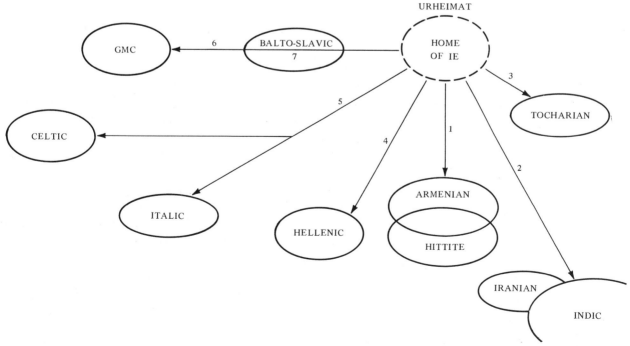

THE GERMANIC BRANCH OF INDO-EUROPEAN

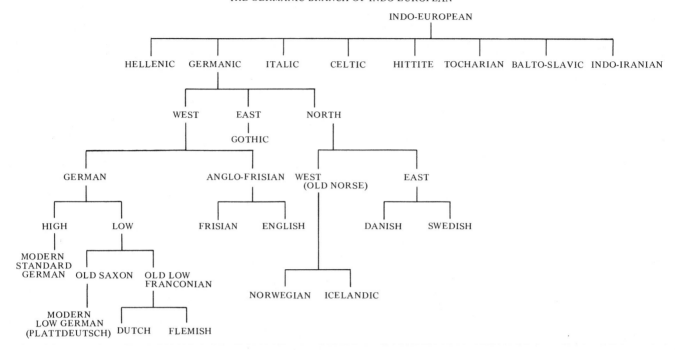

southeast. Virtually all extant Old English literature was written in the West Saxon dialect and dates from about the year 700 and following. The language changed so much by 1050 or 1100 that from that time on to about 1450 or 1500 we refer to it as Middle English.

SOUND CHANGES IN THE PRE–OLD ENGLISH PERIOD

In order to understand the nature of Old English and of its subsequent developments into Middle English and Modern English, the student should be familiar with a few special sound changes dating from the pre-Old English period.

THE GERMANIC PERIOD

GRIMM'S LAW (FIRST CONSONANT SHIFT)[1]

About 1000–400 B.C., a series of consonant changes took place in a certain segment of Primitive Indo-European which was so distinctive that we may say it marked the beginning of Primitive Germanic. All the Germanic languages (and *only* the Germanic languages) reflect these changes. The result is that some non-Germanic words are quite similar to Germanic words except for the changes explained by Grimm's Law. The cause of the shift is unknown, but the most probable theory, the SUBSTRATUM THEORY, suggests that a group of non-Indo-European speakers, in learning to speak Indo-European, substituted their own sounds for sounds unfamiliar to them, and thus modified the language they were learning. Perhaps there were no aspirated stops in their speech, for example, so that they changed the Indo-European aspirated stops to voiced continuants, thus setting the whole system of consonant shifts in motion.

[1] So named because it was formulated (in 1822) by the German philologist, Jacob Grimm. The use of the term "law" here is quite different from that in the physical sciences. In the latter, a law is predictive; in historical linguistics, a law is descriptive only, and the phenomenon it describes occurs only once.

Summary of Grimm's Law

Sound Change		*IE*	*Gmc*
(1) IE aspirated voiced stops	> Gmc voiced continuants	bh, dh, gh	> β, ð, ɣ [later = b, d, g]
(2) IE voiceless stops	> Gmc voiceless continuants	p, t, k	> f, θ, x [later = h, initially]
(3) IE voiced stops	> Gmc voiceless stops	b, d, g	> p, t, k

Examples

(1) bh > β

    Skr *bhrắtār*; OE *brōþor*
        (via Gmc **β–*)

    Skr *bhárāmi*; OE *bere*
        (via Gmc **β–*)

dh > ð

    Lat *medius* (< O Lat *medhios*); OE *mid*
        (via Gmc **–ð*)

    Skr *rudhirá*; OE *rēad*
        (via Gmc **–ð*)

gh > ɣ

    Lat *longus* (< O Lat *longhos*); OE *lang*
        (via Gmc **–ɣ*)

    Lat *ānser* (< O Lat *ghānser*); OE *gōs*
        (via Gmc **ɣ–*)

(2) p > f

    Lat *pater*; OE *fæder*
    Lat *caput*; OE *hēafod*
    Lat *piscis*; OE *fisc*

t > θ

    Lat *tres*; OE *þrīe*
    Lat *frāter*; OE *brōþor*
    Lat *tū*; OE *þū*

k > x

    Lat *centum*; OE *hund*
    Lat *pecus*; OE *feoh*
    Lat *cornu*; OE *horn*

(3) b > p

    Lat *labium*; OE *lippa*
    Lat *turba*; OE *þorp*

d > t

    Lat *duo*; OE *twā, tū*
    Lat *edō*; OE *etan*
    Lat *dēns, dentis*; OE *tōþ*

g > k

    Lat *ego*; OE *iç*
    Lat *genū*; OE *cnēo*
    Lat *ager*; OE *æcer*

Each of the above sets of changes took place before the next set of changes began, and each occurred in the order given. (The letters used, of course, represent sounds.) Notice that not all consonants were affected.[2]

The three rules given above constitute Grimm's Law. The examples following them are not meant to suggest that the English words cited are derived from Sanskrit and Latin forms. They assuredly are not. The English, Sanskrit, and Latin words are linguistic "cousins" of sorts: they are related ("cognate"), but no one of them is the progenitor of the others. Again, all Indo-European languages were originally one language with a common vocabulary and sound system. As each subgroup of Indo-European speakers left the Urheimat, their language developed its own peculiarities, unaffected by the language developments of the other subgroups from whom they were geographically separated. Grimm's Law explains some of the peculiarities of Primitive Germanic and its derivative languages. Thus the original Indo-European form of the word for "father" developed in the Italic group of languages into the classical Latin form *pater*, whereas the same original word developed quite independently in the Germanic group into Old English *fæder*. The Latin word did not come first and the Old English word develop from it: the two words developed independently alongside one another. They may be said to be COGNATE WORDS.

    [2] The sounds referred to in the first stage of Grimm's Law need special comment. The symbols *bh*, *dh*, and *gh* are similar to the [b], [d], [g] sounds represented by the letters *b, d, g*, except that when the lips are released in making the [b] and the tongue released from the roof of the mouth in making the [d] and [g], there is a sudden and marked aspiration or explosion of breath. The β sound, not found in MnE, may be approximated by trying to pronounce [b] without allowing the lips to meet. The symbol ð represents the *th* sound in *then*, and ɣ (not found in MnE) the *g* sound in German *tragen*. In the second stage, the symbol *x* represents the *ch* in German *nacht* or *ich* (not found in MnE).

Related words in two languages are called cognate if they are directly and independently derived in both forms of speech from an earlier form of speech which is the common ancestor of the two.[3]

The examples explaining Grimm's Law could be drawn from many other languages. English is chosen as the representative of the Germanic group obviously because of the student's familiarity with it. Latin forms are used whenever possible to illustrate the lack of the consonant shift in the non-Germanic groups of languages, since it is less exotic than many languages and since it developed roughly (albeit very roughly) at the same time Old English did. The main value of Grimm's Law for the modern student of English is that it helps him understand the proper relationship between such different languages as Latin (and therefore its derivatives Spanish, French, Rumanian, Portuguese, Italian) and English, which belong to two different branches of the Indo-European family tree. English is sometimes said to be closely related to Latin grammatically. It is not. The vocabularies of the two languages are similar, but that is because of the wholesale borrowing from French in the Middle English period (and to a lesser extent in all later periods) and because of borrowing from Latin in various periods, especially during the English Renaissance.

VERNER'S LAW

Sometime after the First Consonant Shift had taken place, several other consonant changes occurred which are explained by Verner's Law. About 1875, the Danish scholar Karl Verner noticed that there seemed to be certain apparent exceptions to Grimm's Law. Why, for example, does the *d* in English *hun*d*red* exist alongside the *t* in Latin *centum*? According to Grimm's Law, one would expect Old English *þ* (=*th*) instead of *d*. Verner explained that when Grimm's Law began to operate, words were stressed according to the Indo-European system, i.e., the main stress was frequently final or medial rather than on the root syllable. (Later the main stress was fairly well stabilized in Germanic languages on the root syllable, usually the first.) He agreed with Grimm that the Indo-European voiceless stops [p, t, k] changed to voiceless continuants [f, θ, x] in Early Primitive Germanic and that this change took place in all positions of the words. However, Verner pointed out that whereas the [f, θ, x] that occurred initially or immediately after a stressed vowel remained [f, θ, x], the same sounds in any other position became voiced continuants [β, ð, ɣ] as Primitive Germanic continued to develop. (Later [β, ð, ɣ] appear historically as [b, d, g].) [s] is similarly voiced to [z] (later [r]). For example, let us look at the development of IE *t* > Gmc *ð* (before a stressed syllable) as compared to IE *t* > Gmc θ (following a stressed syllable). Note also that initial Germanic *f* (< IE *p*) remained *f* because it was initial.

IE *pətér* ——→ Skr *pitár*, Gk *patér*

 'father' ——→ Gmc *faθér* > *faðér* > *fáðer* (>OE *fader* >OE *fæder*)

---

[3] This definition is only slightly modified from that often given to his students by Professor E. V. K. Dobbie. Notice that English words *borrowed* from Latin in historical times (e.g., *alienate*, *dexterity*) are not "cognate" with these Latin forms.

IE *bhráter ⟶ Skr bhrátār
    'brother'
          ⟶ Gmc *βróθōr (> OE brōþor)

SUMMARY OF
VERNER'S LAW

The voiceless continuants [f, θ, s] which resulted from the First Consonant Shift, together with [s] from Indo-European [s], were voiced to [β, ð, ɣ] and [z] everywhere *except*:

1. initially
2. in positions where the immediately preceding vowel had borne the main stress in Indo-European
3. in voiceless surroundings.

Verner's Law manifests itself most clearly in the various parts of the Old English strong verbs (i.e., "irregular" verbs, which form their past tenses by changing the vowel of the root, as in *swim, swam, swum*) in which the infinitive, present participle, present tense, and preterit singular originally had the principal stress on the root syllable, but in which the indicative preterit plural, the preterit subjunctive, and the past participle had the principal stress on the ending. Notice the variation in the principal parts of the following Old English verbs:

inf.	*weorþan*	*ċēosan*	*flēon*
pret. sing.	*wearþ*	*ċēas*	*flēoh*
pret. pl.	*wurdon*	*curon*	*flugon*
past part.	*worden*	*coren*	*flogen*

The most important points to remember about Verner's Law are that it accounts for certain apparent exceptions to Grimm's Law, that it operated sometime after Grimm's Law—although not necessarily a long time afterwards—and especially that it explains many otherwise inexplicable forms in Old English, particularly in the strong verbs, most of which were regularized by analogy later on. Two outstanding irregularities remain in Modern English: the differences between *dead, death* and *was, were*.

THE WEST GERMANIC
PERIOD

GEMINATION

In W Gmc, the combination short vowel+consonant (except *r*)+ *j* resulted in the doubling of the consonant. (Later, the short vowel was mutated [see p. 15], and then the *j* was lost or > ě.)

        cwæljan > OE *cwellan* 'to kill'
        lægjan > OE *leċgan* 'to lay'
          (*g doubled > ċg)
but
        swærjan > OE *swærian* 'to swear'
          (*r* does not geminate, and *j* often > *i*)

LOSS OF NASAL BEFORE VOICELESS CONTINUANTS

In W Gmc, a nasal was lost before a voiceless continuant, and the preceding short vowel was lengthened.

        finf > OE *fīf* 'five'
        uns   > OE *ūs* 'us'
        munþ > OE *mūþ* 'mouth'

SOUND CHANGES IN THE EARLY OLD ENGLISH PERIOD

FRONTING

In very early OE, ă > ǽ everywhere

except
{
(1) before a nasal (where ă sometimes > ŏ)

(2) in open syllables[4] when a back vowel (i.e., *o, u, a*) occurs in the next syllable.
}

> *staf* > OE *stæf* 'staff'
> *dag* > OE *dæg* 'day'

but

> *nama* remained OE *nama* 'name'
>   (ă is before a nasal)
> *stafas* remained OE *stafas* (pl. of *stæf*) and > MnE *staves*
>   (the ă is in an open syllable before another syllable with a back vowel).

BREAKING

In early OE (after fronting had occurred), ǽ, ĕ, ĭ were diphthongized to *ea, eo, io*, respectively,

before
{
l + C (exception: ĕ, ĭ before *l* broke only when a *c* or *h* followed the *l*)

r + C

h + C

h
}

> *hældan* > OE *healdan* 'to hold'
> *melc*   > OE *meolc* 'milk'
> *selh*   > OE *seolh* 'seal'
> *berg*   > OE *beorg* 'hill'
> *liht*   > OE *lioht* 'light, not heavy'
> *sæh*   > OE *seah* 'I saw'

but

> *meltan* remained OE *meltan* 'to melt'
> *delfan* remained OE *delfan* 'to delve'

DIPHTHONGIZATION BY INITIAL PALATALIZATION

Somewhat later in OE, but before the literary period, after initial *ç–, g̣–*, and *sc–*, the vowels ǽ, ĕ, ǣ > *ea, ie, ēa*, respectively.

> *çæster* > OE *çeaster* 'city'
> *sceran* > OE *scieran* 'to cleave'
> *g̣ǣr*   > OE *g̣ēar* 'year'

---

[4] An open syllable is a syllable which ends with a vowel, and a closed syllable is a syllable which ends with a consonant. A single consonant, unless final, belongs to the syllable following it: syllable division occurs between two consonants or a double consonant. Thus, *hūse* has two open syllables and *from* is a closed syllable. *Sumre* consists of a closed syllable and an open syllable, as does * þonne*.

i/j MUTATION (i/j UMLAUT)

(Since these changes occurred before the historical OE period, they are presented here, but the student can best remember the specific mutations after he has studied the OE vowel system on the following pages.) Sometime around the sixth century, certain stressed radical vowels (vowels which occurred in root syllables) and all the diphthongs in OE were mutated (changed) if *i* or *j* occurred in the next syllable. The following diagram (in which the OE long-vowel and short-vowel triangles are combined) shows that mutation occurred in all the vowels to the right of the heavy line (i.e., all the back vowels and one low front vowel, *ӗ*). It also makes clear that the vowels moved in general toward the front of the mouth. Short and long *ŭ* did not entirely front to *ĭ*, but became instead high front rounded *y̆*. After causing mutation, the *i/j* was either lost or became *ĕ*. (After a single *r* preceded by a short vowel or short diphthong, *j* was retained as *ĭ*.) Although not shown on the diagram, all diphthongs became *ĭe* by this sound change (later *ĭ*, *y̆*).

i/j Mutation

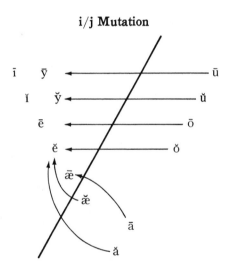

For example, prehistoric OE **manni* > OE *men(n)* 'men'; the *–i* was not present in the early nominative singular form, however, so that OE *man(n)*, nominative singular, exists alongside OE *men(n)*, nominative plural—a distinction which has persisted. Other similar pairs of words, whose differing radical vowels are to be similarly explained, are as follows:

OE	(beside)	OE
mūs 'mouse'		*mȳs* 'mice'
full 'full'		*fyllan* 'to fill'
fōda 'food'		*fēdan* 'to feed'
tōþ 'tooth'		*tēþ* 'teeth'
gōs 'goose'		*gēs* 'geese'
cū 'cow'		*cȳ* 'kine'
hāl 'healthy'; cf. *hale, whole*		*hǣlan* 'to heal'

THE OLD ENGLISH PERIOD

Because of the absence of tape or phonograph recordings, we will never know just how speakers in earlier periods of English history talked. The purpose here is to give approximations based on a broad scholarly consensus, insofar as such a consensus is possible. Scholars agree substantially more about the sounds of Old English and Middle English than about those of Early Modern English, but they do not agree on all of the details (e.g., the quality of the diphthongs). This does not necessarily mean that we know what the language sounded like, however; it just means that there is a textbook solution to the problem.

The most plentiful and the most important type of evidence about early pronunciation is spelling, which tends to represent the actual sounds more systematically than in Modern English. Unfortunately, writing is more conservative than the spoken word, so that there is a "spelling lag"; in fact, spelling is often a more reliable guide about inflections than it is about pronunciation. Dialect spelling is sometimes very important. The speech of Chaucer's two Cambridge students in "The Reeve's Tale" is a good example of dialect spelling in the Middle English period.

Another type of evidence is afforded by the history of languages closely related to English. Knowledge of the development of a German word, for instance, might very well throw light on the history of an English cognate word. After the Old English period, a knowledge of the history of French is desirable. English and French are not very closely related structurally, but English speakers borrowed many French words. A Chaucerian needs to know, for example, that when an Old French word like *juge* 'judge' was borrowed, the initial French sound had not yet become the *z* sound in modern *azure*. Rhymes provide still another type of evidence about the pronunciation of Middle English and Early Modern English words, but rhyme evidence should be used with caution, since writers may or may not, for various reasons, rhyme perfectly. Old English poetry, of course, doesn't rhyme.

It is not difficult to learn to pronounce Old English, since in most cases there is a one-to-one relationship between letters and sounds, and often between letters and IPA symbols. Spelling is not consistent in the Old English texts, however. Inconsistency may result from dialectical variations, idiosyncrasies in scribal pronunciation, or scribal inattentiveness; perhaps it may reflect a groping for a standard orthography. In general, every letter represents a sound, and heavy stress is usually on the first syllable. When the prefixes *ge–*, *be–*, *for–* occur, however, primary stress is on the syllable immediately following, and a compound verb (consisting either of two words combined or of a simple verb with a prefix) is stressed on the first syllable of the second element of the compound.

OLD ENGLISH VOWELS AND DIPHTHONGS

Most of the IPA symbols in the chart on the facing page are explained on pp. 7–8; for modern equivalents of examples given, see p. 33. The rules for pronouncing Old English vowels and diphthongs are as follows:

(1) Long vowels are pronounced according to the modern Continental system. A long vowel is one which is held longer than a short vowel and in phonetic notation is followed by a colon. The distinction is unimportant in MnE, but it is a very distinctive feature of OE. OE long and short

	Seven Long Vowels			*Seven Short Vowels*			*Six Diphthongs*
ī [iː]	ȳ [yː]	ū [uː]	ĭ [ɪ]	ў̆ [ʏ]	ŭ [ʊ]	ēa [æːə] *strēam*
rīdan	*fȳr*	*hūs*	*drincan*	*fyllan*	*under*	ea [æə] *healf*
						ēo [eːo] *dēop*
ē [eː]		ō [oː]	ĕ [ɛ]		ŏ [ɔ]	eo [ɛo] *heorte*
swēte		*fōda*	*helpan*		*oxa*	ĭo [iːo, ɪo] ⎫⁵
ǣ [æː]			æ̆ [æ]			ĭe [iːə, ɪə] ⎭
clǣne			*þæt*			
ā [ɑː]			ă [ɑ]			
stān			*crabba*			

vowels also differ in quality. OE short vowels are very similar to their MnE equivalents (see examples on p. 33). Notice the OE letter æ̆, which was subsequently lost. The sound it represents is one of the sounds the letter *a* represents in MnE.

(2) There is no schwa [ə] vowel sound, except as the second element in some diphthongs. Thus, final –ĕ = [ɛ].

(3) Short and long ў̄ (the letters) represent high front rounded sounds subsequently lost in English, but heard today in French *une* and in the German umlauted *ü* in *über*. OE long ȳ [yː] is held longer than short ў̆ [ʏ], and is perhaps more tense (i.e., the mouth is in the configuration for long ī [iː], with lips rounded, whereas short ў̆ [ʏ] requires the configuration for short ĭ [ɪ], with lips rounded). In late OE, the letters *i* and *y* are often used interchangeably, indicating a breakdown of the phonetic distinction. (See p. xii, above.)

(4) OE diphthongs are "falling" diphthongs: i.e., the first element of each diphthong is heavily stressed, so that the voice falls off as the second element is pronounced.

OLD ENGLISH CONSONANTS The letters *j, q, š,* and *z* do not occur in OE, and *k* and *x* appear very rarely. The letter *w* is often written *u, uu,* or ƿ (called a "wen," also "wyn" or "wynn"). This and most other consonants are pronounced as in MnE, with the following exceptions.

(1) The letters *f, s,* and *þ/ð* (*þ* and *ð* are interchangeable in the spelling) are voiceless [f, s, θ] initially, finally, and in voiceless surroundings, and are voiced [v, z, ð] in voiced surroundings (i.e., intervocalically and between a vowel and a voiced consonant).

(2) The letter *c* represents an ordinary velar or palatal [k] (the distinction will come automatically, as in MnE, depending on the nature of the sound following), except when it is [č]. Generally, *c* = [k] when adjacent to back vowels (*boc* 'book', *camp* 'battle'), and [č] when adjacent to front vowels. The pronunciation of MnE equivalents may be used as a test. More specifically, [č] occurs in the following instances (elsewhere *c* = [k]):

      a) initially before ĕ, ĭ, or a diphthong (*çild* 'child', *çēosan* 'to choose', *çeorl* 'peasant')

      b) finally after ĭ (*iç* 'I', *sārlīç* 'painful')

      c) medially between ĭ and a front vowel (*rīçe* 'kingdom', *luflīçe* 'gladly')

---

⁵ These sounds do not often appear in our late OE texts, where they have usually become ĕo and ĭ/ў̆, respectively.

d) when originally followed by *ĭ* or *j*, subsequently lost (*sēçan* 'to seek', *çiriçe* 'church')

As a rule of thumb, if the word in which the sound appears has survived into MnE, the OE *c* is palatal if it is still palatal in MnE. In this text, a dot is placed under palatal *ç*.

(3) The pronunciation represented by the letter *g* (written ȝ in OE texts) is the most troublesome sound in OE, and modern scholars do not agree with one another about it. In this text it will be said to represent three sounds, although the beginning student may ignore the difference between [g] and [ɣ], which is hard to pronounce, and consider them both [g].

(a) *g* = [g] a voiced velar stop, usually initial. It appears before consonants, initially before back vowels, initially before front vowels resulting from mutated back vowels, and in the combination *ng* (*gnæt* 'gnat', *gos* 'goose', *ges* < **gosi* 'geese', *hring* 'ring'). In general, OE *g* is [g] if the word in which it survives into MnE has [g], for example, *gylt* > *guilt*.

(b) *g* = [j], a voiced fronto-palatal glide, usually in the presence of front vowels. It occurs initially before *ĕ*, *ĭ*, or a diphthong; medially between front vowels; finally, or at the end of a syllable before a front vowel; or when followed prehistorically by *ĭ* or *j* (*ġeslēan* 'to strike', *ġieldan* 'to yield', *twegen* 'twain', *weġ* 'way', *bīeġan* 'to bend'). Notice that OE [j] frequently remains a glide in MnE (*mæġ* > *may*, *hāliġ* > *holy*). In this text, a dot is placed under palatal *g*.

(c) *g* = [ɣ], a voiced velar fricative, in other positions. This sound is not found in MnE, but is to be heard in German *tragen*. In OE, it often occurs after or between back vowels and may > ME *w* [w] (*dagas* 'days', *lagu* 'law', *sorgian* 'to sorrow').

As a rule of thumb, except when [j], *g* = [g] initially (and in the combination *ng*) and [ɣ] medially or finally.

(4) In the combination *–ng–*, the *g* is pronounced [g], whereas in MnE it is usually silent, and the *–n–* is pronounced [ŋ] (as in MnE): *singan* [sɪŋgɑn] 'to sing'.

(5) In the combination *–nc–*, the *n* is pronounced [ŋ]: *sincan* [sɪŋkɑn] 'to sink'.

(6) Initially, the letter *h* represents the same sound [h] as it does in MnE. Otherwise, it represents the voiceless fricative [x], which does not occur in MnE, but which may be heard in Modern German *ich* [ɪx] 'I'.

(7) The letters *–çg–* represent the affricate [ǰ] sound of *–dg–* in MnE *edge*: *eçg* [ɛǰ] 'edge'.

(8) The letters *sc* are pronounced [š]: *scip* [šɪp] 'ship'.

(9) The letter *r* represents a highly tongue-trilled sound.

(10) Double consonants represent long consonants, meaning that they are held longer than a single consonant is (cf. MnE *penknife*). In phonetic notation, a long consonant is followed by a colon.

IMPORTANT OLD ENGLISH DIALECT VARIATIONS

As the accompanying map shows, there were four OE dialects. Most surviving OE texts were written in West Saxon, which became the standard literary dialect. It is important to note a few features of the other dialects, however, since many ME and MnE forms are not derived from West Saxon. For geographical reasons, Chaucer's ME dialect, which becomes

OLD ENGLISH DIALECTS

standard EMnE, developed out of Mercian and was sometimes influenced by other OE dialects. It would be difficult at times, therefore, to trace words back to their OE forms if we did not remember several important features about the various OE dialects. Fortunately, the OE dialects were, in general, very similar.

(1) A small but important group of ME words comes from Mercian $\breve{a}$, lengthened to $\bar{a}$ in late OE before $-ld$:

$$\begin{array}{rcl} \text{Mercian } \bar{a}ld & > & \text{ME } \bar{\phi}ld \\ b\bar{a}ld & > & b\bar{\phi}ld \\ w\bar{a}ld & > & w\bar{\phi}ld \\ c\bar{a}ld & > & c\bar{\phi}ld \end{array}$$

Since the West Saxon forms were spelled with ea, they could not have developed into MnE as the forms we know.

(2) The diphthongs $\breve{\imath}e$ and $\bar{\imath}e$ occurred only in West Saxon. In Mercian, we find $\bar{e}$ instead of West Saxon $\bar{\imath}e$.

West Saxon $st\bar{\imath}eran$ 'to direct'⎱
⎰ but ⎱ Mercian $st\bar{e}ran > steer$

$st\bar{\imath}epel$ 'steeple'⎰ ⎱ $st\bar{e}pel > steeple$

(3) In Anglian (i.e., Mercian and Northumbrian), we find $\bar{e}$ instead of the West Saxon diphthongs $\bar{e}a$ and $\bar{e}o$:

West Saxon $\bar{e}ac$ 'also'⎱
⎰ but ⎱ Mercian & Northumb. $\bar{e}c > \text{ME } \bar{\phi}k$

$l\bar{e}ac$ 'leek'⎰ ⎱ $l\bar{e}c > l\bar{\phi}k$

(4) In Chaucer's works, many words have e where i might be expected. The reason is that Old Kentish has $\bar{e}$ where West Saxon has $\bar{\ae}$ and $\bar{y}$, and has $\breve{e}$ where West Saxon has $\breve{\ae}$ and $\breve{y}$. Some of these Old Kentish words made their way into Chaucer's works. Some MnE words are derived from Old Kentish forms:

$$\begin{array}{rcl} \text{MnE } knell & < & \text{Old Kentish } cnellan \\ hemlock & < & heml\bar{\imath}\c{c} \\ merry & < & meri\c{g} \end{array}$$

(5) Historically, there are two kinds of $\bar{\ae}$ in OE: $\bar{\ae}^1$ and $\bar{\ae}^2$. In West Saxon, they are both spelled $\bar{\ae}$. Historically, $\bar{\ae}^1 < $ W Gmc $*\bar{a}$, and $\bar{\ae}^2 < $ i-mutation of Early OE $*\bar{a} < $ W Gmc $*ai$. West Saxon $\bar{\ae}^1 = $ Mercian $\bar{e}$, which develops regularly into Chaucer's $\bar{\phi}$ [eː].

		West Saxon	
W Gmc	*Early OE*	*(after i-mutation)*	*Mercian*
$\bar{a}$	$\bar{\ae}^1$	$\bar{\ae}^1$	$\bar{e}$
ai	$\bar{a}$	$\bar{\ae}^2$	$\bar{\ae}^2$

In MnE, $\bar{\ae}^1$ is spelled ee (or ie) [i]; modern cognates in German are spelled a [ɑ], e.g., OE $d\bar{\ae}d$, $str\bar{\ae}t$, $sl\bar{\ae}p$, $s\bar{\ae}d$ beside MnE $deed$, $street$, $sleep$, $seed$ and German Tat, $Strasse$, $Schlaf$, $Saat$. In MnE, $\bar{\ae}^2$ is spelled ea; cognates in German are frequently spelled ei, e.g., OE $l\bar{\ae}dan$, $h\bar{\ae}lan$, $s\bar{\ae}$, $cl\bar{\ae}ne$ beside MnE $lead$, $heal$, sea, $clean$ and German $leiten$, $heilen$, See, $klein$.

vowel lengthening before -ld, -nd, -mb

THE MIDDLE ENGLISH PERIOD

VOWELS: SOUND CHANGES IN THE LATE OLD ENGLISH AND EARLY MIDDLE ENGLISH PERIODS

LENGTHENING BEFORE *-ld*, *-nd*, *mb* IN LATE OLD ENGLISH

In late Old English, short vowels lengthened before certain voiced homorganic consonant groups[6]—especially *–ld*, *–nd*, *–mb*.

> Early OE *ald* > Late OE *āld* (> ME *ǭld* > MnE *old*)
> Early OE *feld* > Late OE *fēld* (> ME *fẹld* > MnE *field*)
> Early OE *çild* > Late OE *çīld* (> ME *chīld* > MnE *child*)

The following Late OE forms may similarly be accounted for:

> *blīnd* (> MnE *blind*)
> *fīndan* (> MnE *find*)
> *grūnd* (> MnE *ground*)
> *cāmb* (> MnE *comb*)
> *clīmban* (> MnE *climb*)

EXCEPTIONS

(1) *End, send, hand, land, dumb*, among others, apparently did not show lengthening, as we can tell by their "short" sounds in MnE.

(2) When a third consonant followed, the vowel did not lengthen; thus while the vowel in *çild* lengthened, it remained short in *çildru*—a distinction which persists in MnE *child, children*. Also compare the MnE pronunciation of *hound* with that of *hundred* (*hund* > Late OE *hūnd* and later *hound*, but the *–ndr–* combination in OE *hundred* prevented lengthening).

SHORTENING IN EARLY MIDDLE ENGLISH

long vowels shortened

$$[\underset{+long}{V}] \rightarrow [-long] / \_\_ CC \text{ (in past tense)}$$

In EME, long vowels were shortened

1. before two consonants or before a double consonant—a change noticeable in the past tense of certain weak verbs, accounting for the difference in vowel sounds between MnE *meet, met*; *hide, hid*; *keep, kept*.

> OE *mētan, mētte* (beside) ME *mẹte(n), mette*
> OE *hȳdan, hȳdde* (beside) ME *hīde(n), hidde*
> OE *cēpan, cēpte* (beside) ME *kẹpe(n), kepte*

Similar distinctions are apparent in

> MnE *stone* (< OE *stān*) beside *Stanford*
> MnE *goose* (< OE *gōs*) beside *gosling*
> MnE *wise* (< OE *wīs*) beside *wisdom*

2. in the first syllables of trisyllabic words.

> MnE *south* (< OE *sūþ*) beside MnE *southern* (< OE *sūþerne*)
> MnE *out* (< OE *ūt*) beside MnE *utter* (< OE *ūterra*, originally meaning 'outer')
> MnE *holy* (< OE *hālig*) beside MnE *Halifax* (< OE *Hāligfeax*), and MnE *halibut* (< OE *hāligbut*)

[6] Homorganic consonants are consonants formed in the same place in the mouth in similar but not identical ways.

3.   in unstressed syllables.

> MnE *town* (< OE *tūn*) beside MnE *Kingstown / Kingston*
> (< OE *Kingestūn*)

LENGTHENING OF *ă*, *ĕ*, *ŏ* IN EARLY MIDDLE ENGLISH

Around the thirteenth century, ME *ă*, *ĕ*, *ŏ* lengthened in open syllables of disyllabic words.

> OE *năma* (beside) ME *nāme* ('name')
> OE *ĕtan* (beside) ME *ẹ̄te(n)* ('to eat')
> OE *ŏpen* (beside) ME *ǭpen* ('open')

REGULAR VOWEL
CHANGES: OLD ENGLISH
TO MIDDLE ENGLISH

The ME vowel system may best be understood first by comparing the OE and ME vowel triangles and then by listing and commenting upon the specific changes.

	OE Long Vowels			*ME Long Vowels*	
ī ȳ		ū	ī		ū
	ē		ō	ẹ̄	ǭ
		ǣ		ę̄	ǭ
	ā			ā	

	OE Short Vowels			*ME Short Vowels*	
ĭ y̆		ŭ	ĭ		ŭ
	ĕ		ŏ	ĕ	ŏ
	æ̆				
	ă			ă	

Notice that OE *ā* was raised and retracted to ME *ǭ*. This change did not result in the absence of ME *ā*, however, which developed, as we have seen, from the lengthening of *ă* in open syllables of disyllabic words and also from the borrowing of certain French words whose vowels, although not long or short in French, were assigned length according to the English system (e.g., OF *dame*, whose *a* was treated as a long vowel in English, since it occurred in an open syllable of a disyllabic word). This increase by one in the number of ME long vowels was offset by the falling together of OE *ȳ* with *ī*. OE *ǣ* changed in quality to *ẹ̄*, but there were still seven long vowels in ME.

The short vowels remained the same, except that OE *y̆* fell together with *ĭ* and OE *æ̆* with *ă*. In addition, when short *ĕ* occurred in completely un-stressed positions, it was reduced to [ə]. The schwa sound of final un-

	Old English		Middle English
Spelling	*Sound*	*Spelling*	*Sound*
ī ȳ	[iː] [yː] ⟩ ī, ȳ		[iː][7]
ĭ y̆	[ɪ] [ʏ] ⟩ ĭ, y̆		[ɪ]
ē ēo	[eː] [eːo] ⟩ ẹ̄, ẹẹ		[eː]
ĕ ĕo	[ɛ] [ɛo] ⟩ ĕ		[ɛ]
ǣ ēa	[æː] [æːə] ⟩ ę̄, ęę		[ɛː]
æ̆ ĕa	[æ] [æə] ⟩ ă		[a]
ū	[uː]	ū, ou ow	[uː]
ŭ	[ʊ]	ŭ, ŏ	[ʊ]
ō	[oː]	ọ̄, ọọ	[oː]
ŏ	[ɔ]	ŏ	[ɔ]
ā	[ɑː]	ǭ, ǫǫ	[ɔː]
ă	[ɑ]	ă	[a]

Marginal/handwritten notes:

SE Midland (Chaucer) [ɛː]

[eː]
SE (Kent, Essex) = standard development

#7 p. 71

[ʊ] come honey tongue love monk

[+̆ long] → V V / ___ C (closed)

[+̆ long] → V / ___ (open)

stressed –ĕ is a very prominent feature of ME poetry, although by Chaucer's time final –ĕ might have been silent for metrical purposes. Indeed in ordinary speech and in prose, it was probably lost before Chaucer.

Notice that the letter *o* represents four sounds in ME, including [ʊ] in words like *come, love, wonder, honey, monk, tongue*. These words all had *ŭ* in OE, but were subsequently respelled with *ŏ*, since before *n, m,* or *v* the handwritten *u* was hard to distinguish.

Notice also that the letter *e* represents three sounds in ME. Words with ME [ɛː][8] are usually spelled –*ea*– or *e . . . e* in MnE (*clean, mete*), and words with ME [eː] are usually spelled –*ee*– or –*ie*– in MnE (*deep, field*).

In ME there is no reliable distinction in spelling between long and short vowels. However, scribes often doubled the long vowel in closed syllables. Compare the spellings of the short vowels [a, ɛ, ɔ] in *fat, bed, lok* with those of the long vowels [ɑː, eː, ɛː, oː, ɔː] in *caas, dẹẹd* (> *deed*), *dęęd* (> *dead*), *stọọd, stǫǫn*, respectively. In open syllables, however, a long vowel is frequently written as a single vowel (ME *lẹde(n)* 'to lead', *mẹte(n)* 'to meet'). After a short vowel, the consonant is sometimes doubled, unless the consonant is final.

---

[7] In the phonetic transcription of ME in Part Two, a modification of this sound, [ɨ], is used in certain unstressed syllables of words like *diversity* [dɪvɛrsɨteː] and *any* [ɛnɨ]. The sound is the same sound heard in most modern American speech in the final syllables of words like *city* [sɪtɨ] and *pretty* [prɪtɨ]. (In southern speech, the pronunciation is often [ɪ].)

[8] The complex development of ME [ɛː] is explained later, pp. 29 ff.

MIDDLE ENGLISH DIPHTHONGS

As the list on p. 23 shows, OE diphthongs were monothongized. Five other diphthongs developed, however, from OE sounds, and one entirely new diphthong *oi/oy* [ɔɪ] was introduced into ME in French borrowings such as *annoy, joy, soil, toil*. In general, the native ME diphthongs most frequently resulted from the following OE combinations:

a front vowel or a diphthong + *ġ* [j] or *w* [w]

or

a back vowel + *g* [ɣ], *w* [w], *h* [x], or *ht* [xt].

ME diphthongs

1. [æɪ], *ei, ai, ey, ay*:

tweye < OE *twegen*
dai < OE *dæg*
wey < OE *weg*
pleie < OE *plega* [plɛɣɑ]
neighebour < EME *nehhebur*

Note: in EME, *ai* and *ei* represent two separate diphthongs, but they represent identical sounds by Chaucer's time.

2. [ɔʊ], *ǫu, ǫw*:

grǫwe(n) < OE *grōwan*
blǫwe(n) < OE *blāwan*
ǫwen < OE *āgen* [ɑɪɣɛn]
bǫwe < OE *boga* [bɔɣɑ]
bǫugh < OE *bōh*
twǫwe(n) < OE *trēowian*
bǫughte < OE *bohte*

3. [ɑʊ], *au, aw*:

clawe < OE *clawe*
drawe(n) < OE *dragan* [drɑɣɑn]
faught < OE *fæht* (Mercian)
taughte < OE *tāhte*

4. [ɛʊ], *ęu, ęw*:

dęwe < OE *dēaw*
lęwed < OE *lǣwed*

5. [iʊ], *iu, iw, u*:

stiward < OE *stigweard/stīweard*
bręwe(n) < OE *brēowan*
vertu, whose final sound was [–yː] in the OF original, anglicized into [iʊ] when the word was borrowed

6. [ɔɪ], *oi, oy*:

joie (OF)

MIDDLE ENGLISH CONSONANTS

(1) Every letter generally represents a sound in ME, except *h* in French words like *honour* and in short words like *he* and *him* in unstressed position.

(2) When pronounced, initial *h–* = [h–], as in OE and MnE. In other positions, *h* may occur in the combination *–gh–*, which is pronounced [x], as *–h–* is in OE. OE *hw–* was respelled *wh–*, but still pronounced [hw–]. Initial *h–* was lost in the combinations *hr–, hl–, hn–*.

(3) The letters *f*, *s*, and *th*, as in OE, are normally voiceless [f, s, θ] initially and finally, and are normally voiced [v, z , ð] between vowels.[9] Because of French influence, however, words with initial letters *v* and *z* (*vair, zeal*) now come into the language and are pronounced with [v–] and [z–], sounds which did not occur initially in OE. Presumably, the voicing of initial *th–* occurs after Chaucer's time, although it may already have occurred by Chaucer's time in short, common words like *the, there, this*.

(4) OE *ç* was respelled *ch*, due to OF influence, but still pronounced [č].

(5) OE *–çç–* was respelled *c(c)h* (> MnE *–tch–*), but still pronounced [čɪ].

(6) OE *–çg–* was respelled *–gg–*, but still pronounced [ǰ].

(7) The letter *g*, often represented *ȝ*, is pronounced [g]. The OE prefix *ge–* disappeared (or was reduced to *i/y*), and the *g* in words like OE *dæg* changed to *i/y* as part of the ME diphthong [æɪ]. OE velar [ɣ] became ME *w* [w] in those words which survived.

(8) The letter *ȝ* represents a variety of sounds, especially [g, j, x].[10]

(9) OE *–ng–* is still pronounced [–ŋg–].

(10) OE *–nc–* was respelled *–nk–*, but still pronounced [–ŋk–].

(11) OE *sc* was respelled *s(s)h* or *sch*, but still pronounced [š].

(12) The letters *j*, *k*, *q*, and *v* occur regularly in ME. (Under French influence, OE *cw–* was respelled *qu–*.) The letters *x* and *z* occur, as in MnE, with relative rarity.

(13) Double consonants are presumably still long.

(14) The letter *r* represents a highly tongue-trilled sound.

MIDDLE ENGLISH STRESS

ME stress patterns are about the same as those in MnE. This is because many Latinate words came into ME, because many OE words were lost, and because OE inflections were largely leveled or reduced. Chaucer had more leeway than later writers like Shakespeare, however, in the pronunciation of French borrowings. For example, he could stress the final syllables of words like *honour* or *citee* if he needed to for metrical purposes.

---

[9] In the prose passages in Part Two, words like *hise, nose, rise, these* and *wise* are transcribed with final [–z]. *Explanation*: It is assumed that final *–e* was lost in speech, and therefore in prose, in the ME period, even though often retained in verse for metrical reasons. In verse, and before it was lost in speech, the intervocalic *–s–* in words like *hise* is assumed to have been voiced; when the *–e* was lost, it is assumed that this *s* remained voiced, especially if it is still voiced in MnE. When these same words are spelled without the final *–e*, however, the final *–s* is assumed to be voiceless. These assumptions produce a certain amount of ambiguity in the transcriptions, but presumably both pronunciations of *s* existed side by side during at least some portion of the ME period.

[10] Sometimes *ȝ* seems to represent the [ɪ] of the diphthong [æɪ], as in *maȝȝ* [mæɪ] 'may'. In *The Ormulum*, a very early ME document, it sometimes seems to represent [ɣ] as well, as in *follȝhenn* [fɔlɣən] 'follow' and *hallȝhe* [hɑlɣə] 'holy'. Sometimes it is impossible to distinguish between the values [g] and [j], as in words like *ȝyue* 'give' and *forȝyue* 'forgive', since both pronunciations seem to have existed side by side.

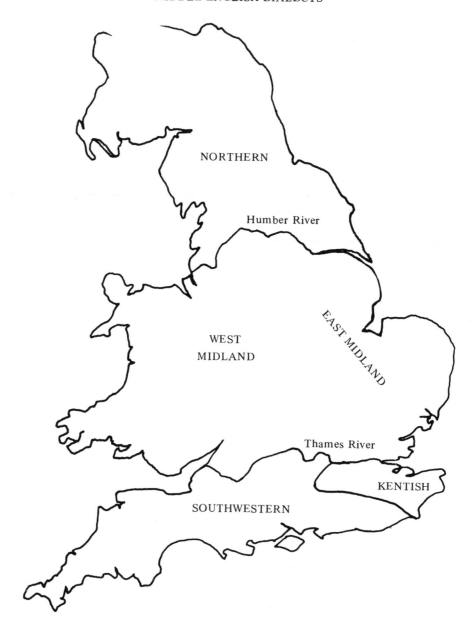

MIDDLE ENGLISH DIALECTS

NORTHERN

Humber River

EAST MIDLAND

WEST
MIDLAND

Thames River

KENTISH

SOUTHWESTERN

MIDDLE ENGLISH DIALECTS

The five main Middle English dialects grew out of the four Old English dialects, as follows:

Northern   < Northumbrian

West Midland ⎫

East Midland ⎭   < Mercian

Southwestern (or Southern) < West Saxon

Kentish (or Southeastern)   < Old Kentish

A few of the important Middle English dialect characteristics follow:[11]

NORTHERN (GREATEST SCANDINAVIAN INFLUENCE HERE)

1. OE *ā* remained [ɑː]
2. *–and* for the present participle
3. *qu* for OE *hw* and for ME non-Northern *wh* (apparently an orthographic feature only)
4. *–es/–is* ending for present indicative plural verb and for third person singular
5. *them, their* instead of *hem, here* for accusative and genitive plural of third person personal pronoun
6. *sal, solde* (*sulde*) instead of *shal, sholde* (as in non-Northern) reflects a distinction between [s], [š]
7. preference for *are* instead of *be* (or *beth*) in present plural of verb "to be"
8. retention of Anglian [k] before front vowels instead of [č], seen in MnE *kirk* for *church*
9. use of ON *at* or *til* for *to* in infinitive

WEST MIDLAND

1. OE *ă* > *ŏ* before *m, n,* except before *–ng, –nd, –mb* (*mon, ronk, nome*)
2. *–eth* (especially in S. West Midland) for present indicative third person singular; *–en* for plural present
3. preference for *–end* in present participle
4. preference for *ho* or *ha* for third person singular feminine pronoun *she*
5. in the S. West Midland, [f] > [v]
6. OE *ў̆* remained rounded front vowel for a long time (spelled *u, ue, ui,* etc.)

SOUTHWESTERN (OR SOUTHERN)

1. voicing of [f] to [v], and [s] to [z] (the latter usually not shown in the spelling)
2. *–ind* for present participle; later *–ing*
3. OE *ў̆* remained rounded
4. *–eth* for present indicative plural verb (and singular)

---

[11] This list is based largely on Moore and Marckwardt, *Historical Outlines*, Chapter 7, which the student may consult for additional dialect features.

KENTISH (OR SOUTHEASTERN)

1. voicing of OE [f] to [v] (*vixen*)
2. *–ind* or *–ing* for present participle
3. preference for *–eth* in present plural of verb (also in present singular)
4. the development of a semivowel glide before *o* in certain words (*guod* for *good*)
5. substitution of *e* for *i* in some words (*pet* for *pit*; *fer* for *fire*)

EAST MIDLAND

1. absence of outstanding features; similarity to MnE
2. use of *–en* for present indicative plural of verbs
3. past participle has no prefix *y–*, but has suffix *–en*

THE EARLY MODERN ENGLISH PERIOD

Before summarizing a few of the more distinctive EMnE characteristics, a word of caution seems necessary. It is difficult to be sure about the pronunciation of a given sound in Shakespeare's London, for the evidence, being so abundant, is quite confusing and often actually contradictory.[12] In the sixteenth century, writers commented extensively on the language for the first time, but their commentary is not always reliable. In an age long before the perfection of an International Phonetic Alphabet, commentators' descriptions of sounds may be highly ambiguous. Some writers have better ears for sounds than others. The dialect of a young man is often somewhat different from that of one considerably older, so that if the two men comment on a given point, they may disagree. Also, their spelling may differ because of some geographical separation.

THE GREAT VOWEL SHIFT

Sometime during the fifteenth century, and for a reason still unknown, the long vowels of English underwent a systematic change known as the Great Vowel Shift (GVS). (See schema on p. 30.) Notice that the result (Fig. 3) was an irregular patterning of long vowels,[13] and that the shift itself involved a general raising in the mouth of all long vowels. Since [iː] and [uː] could be raised no higher, they were diphthongized.[14] Long ā [ɑː] disappeared (the reintroduction and later development of this sound is very complex and need not concern us here) and was apparently not in the speech of Shakespeare's London. Long open ǭ [ɔː] also disappeared. (It was replaced at about the same time, however, by the regular development of the ME diphthong [ɑʊ] (see Fig. 4)—but this development was not part of the GVS.) When we add the long vowel [ɔː] resulting from the regular development of ME [ɑʊ], we have the complete set of EMnE long vowels.

The development of ME long open ę̄ into the modern period was complex and unusual. The following comments should be augmented not only by the schema of the GVS on p. 30, but also by the graphic explanation on p. 33 below. In the Southeast Midland dialect of Chaucer's London, long open ę̄ resisted the GVS and remained ę̄ into the EMnE period, subsequently becoming [eː]; however, only five words in present-day standard English reflect this line of development: *great, yea, break, steak,* and *drain* (whose late spelling change obscures its derivation < ME ę̄). All other words in MnE that are derived from ME ę̄ reflect the development of the sound in the Southeast dialect of Kent and Essex, where ME ę̄ > Late ME ē̜ > EMnE [iː]. These MnE words are normally spelled, like *clean* and *stream,* with *ea*. Thus, ME ę̄ is eventually raised two vowel positions in the mouth, but this raising should not be thought of as part of the GVS.

---

[12] The best modern study of Shakespeare's speech—and it is a very good one—is that by the late Professor Helge Kökeritz (*Shakespeare's Pronunciation,* New Haven, 1953), but even this analysis of the evidence is admittedly not always conclusive.

[13] The absence of the [eː] sound in EMnE is especially noteworthy. Words like *name* <ME [ɑː], *day*<ME [æɪ], and *great* (together with *clean*)<ME [ɛː] are all pronounced with [ɛː], as the chart on p. 33 indicates.

[14] The distinctive diphthongs [əɪ] and [əʊ] may still be heard in the United States in the Tidewater Virginia area and as far north as southern Delaware—regions which begin to be settled shortly after the sound change takes place, and where later changes to [aɪ] and [aʊ] are resisted because of the geographical distance from the mainstream of English sound development.

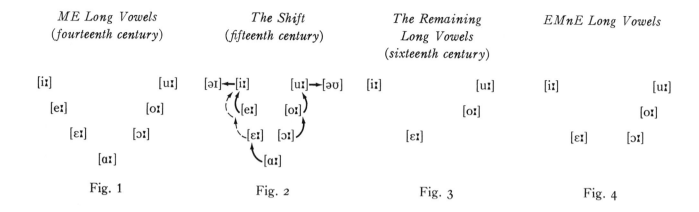

| ME Long Vowels (fourteenth century) | The Shift (fifteenth century) | The Remaining Long Vowels (sixteenth century) | EMnE Long Vowels |

Fig. 1   Fig. 2   Fig. 3   Fig. 4

In Chaucer's time, [eː] exists as a variant of [ɛː], although mainly in different dialects, as the chart on p. 33 shows:

$$\bar{ę},\ ęę\ [\varepsilon\text{ː}] \quad \begin{array}{c} \nearrow\ [\varepsilon\text{ː}] \\ \searrow\ [e\text{ː}] \end{array}$$

As the chart also shows, these sounds developed by Shakespeare's time into [ɛː] and [iː], which were often variants of one another. In fact, it is likely that both pronunciations of words like *clean* and *stream* were current in London.[15]

The development of ME long close ǭ was even more complicated. Fig. 2 above shows that the vowel regularly > [uː] in words like *food*. Following the development of ME ǭ on the chart on p. 33, one can see that in another class of words, represented by *good*, this EMnE [uː] subsequently shortened (after Shakespeare's time) to [ʊ] and remains [ʊ] today in standard English. (This shortening is not part of the GVS.) In still another class of words < ME ǭ, represented by *blood*, the shortening to [ʊ] occurred somewhat earlier in the EMnE period and then changed to [ʌ], still in the EMnE period, and remains [ʌ] today in standard English. So three classes of present-day words, those spelled with –oo– and pronounced with the vowel sounds of *blood*, *good*, and *food*, go back to ME ǭ. (Remember the sentence, "Blood is good food.") For Shakespeare, *good* and *food* probably rhymed, but not with *blood*. For Chaucer, all three words rhymed.

EXCEPTIONAL DEVELOPMENTS OF VOWELS: MIDDLE ENGLISH TO EARLY MODERN ENGLISH

(1) ME ǎ > [æ] usually, but after *w* and before *r* remained [a] or was somewhat raised (*swan, wand, hard, are*), and sometimes it was lengthened. Today, there is considerable variety in the pronunciation of this ǎ.
(2) ME ǎ did not always become [æ] before [f, θ, s, mp, nt, nd, ns, nč], but sometimes remained [a], perhaps lengthened (*half, bath, glass, example, chant, command, dance, branch*).

[15] E. J. Dobson's explanation of the development of ME ę̄ and of the origin of EMnE [iː] differs somewhat from the one outlined here. He argues that the EMnE [iː] pronunciation of ME ę̄ words comes not from an intermediate stage [eː], but from "a late ME ē variant, commonly developed from ME ę̄ in ME times, but often older still.... There was in a sense a change of pronunciation from [eː] to [iː], but it was not a ModE phonetic change; it was simply the displacement of one mode of pronunciation by another which had developed from it before the ModE period began. This theory assumes that all 'ME ę̄ words' had a ME variant in ME ē" (*English Pronunciation, 1500–1700*, Vol. II [Oxford, 1957], pp. 611–612).

(3) ME ę̄ [ɛː] normally remained [ɛː] in EMnE, but was further shortened to [ɛ] in *bread, death, dead, deaf, head, lead, red, wet*. (Note: the same vowel in *every, heaven*, and *weapon* had already shortened by Chaucer's time.)

(4) ME ē̩ [eː] > EMnE [iː], which was then often shortened to EMnE [ɪ] in *been, breeches, sieve*. The alternate MnE pronunciation [i] in *been* and *sieve* suggests that the shortening did not always occur in these words.

(5) ME ŭ remained [ʊ]: *pull, full, push*; or was unrounded to [ʌ]: *but, dull, run*.

(6) ME –ăl finally and before consonants > [–ɑʊl] > Shakespearian [–ɔːl], as in *all*. The ă did not change in the combination ăl+vowel, or before –*lm* in words like *balm, calm, palm*, or before –*lf* in words like *calf, half*.

(7) ME –ĕr > [–ɑr] finally and before consonants (no change occurred before vowels: cf. *error, very*).

> (a) Sometimes respelling eventually occurred (ME *sterre, derke* > *star, dark*).

> (b) Sometimes no respelling occurred (ME *clerk, serve(n)*), and the pronunciation after Shakespeare's day eventually changed again to MnE [ɝ], i.e., ME [ɛr] > EMnE [ɑr] > MnE [ɝ].

> (c) In the case of ME *serjeaunt*, no respelling of the sound occurred, and the pronunciation has not been changed again in MnE, i.e., ME [ɛr] > EMnE [ɑr] > MnE [ɑr].

(8) ME –ĭr, –ŭr, and –ŏr finally and before consonants > [–ɝ]: *bird, burn, worthy*. In Shakespeare, these words do not rhyme with words like *serve* and *clerk*.

EARLY MODERN ENGLISH DIPHTHONGS

As we have seen (pp. 29–30), the EMnE diphthongs [əɪ] and [əʊ] resulted from the GVS, i.e., they correspond to ME [iː] and [uː], respectively. As the chart (p. 33) indicates, [əɪ] also resulted when the ME diphthong [ɔɪ] developed regularly into EMnE as [əɪ]. (ME [ɔɪ] had come from French borrowings like *annoy* and *toil*.) Thus, for Shakespeare, the vowels of both *fire* (< ME [iː]) and *boy* (< ME [ɔɪ]) were [əɪ]. As the chart also indicates, the other EMnE diphthong was [iʊ], which resulted from the regular development and merging of the two ME diphthongs [ɛʊ] and [iʊ]. Thus, Shakespeare had three diphthongs altogether:

[əɪ]
[əʊ]
[iʊ]

EARLY MODERN ENGLISH CONSONANTS

(1) ME –*ti*–, –*ssi*–, –*si*–, –*di*– became the affricates [š], [ž], or [ǰ]:
ME *nation* [nɑːsɪuːn] > EMnE [nɛɪsjən] > EMnE [nɛɪšən]
ME *mission* [mɪsɪuːn] > EMnE [mɪsjən] > EMnE [mɪšən]
ME *vision* [vɪzɪuːn] > EMnE [vɪzjən] > EMnE [vɪžən]
ME *sǭldier* [sɔːldɪer] > EMnE [soːldjɝ] > EMnE [soːljɝ]

It is uncertain whether or not by Shakespeare's time these sounds had progressed, as shown, to the affricates [š, ž, ǰ]. Some variation may have existed in Shakespeare, the affricates occurring perhaps colloquially.

(2) In the combinations *gn*–, *kn*–, the initial [g–] and [k–] of words like *gnaw* and *knight* were probably lost by Shakespeare's time, although we cannot be sure. If they were not lost by that time, they were certainly lost soon afterwards. It is possible that pronunciations with and without [g–] and [k–] existed alongside each other in Shakespeare's speech.

(3) The letter *l* in *could*, although never pronounced, was added to the word by analogy with the *l* in *would* and *should* (< OE *wolde* and *scolde*), although the [l] even in these two words had probably been lost by Shakespeare's time. In words like *calf* and *walk*, it seems best to assume that the pronunciation with the [l] existed alongside the pronunciation without the [l].

(4) *–ing* = [–ɪn] in unstressed positions, as in present participles.

(5) The reduction of weak untrilled *r* (i.e., preconsonental and final) may have begun by Shakespeare's time.

(6) ME [θ] > [ð] in certain unstressed words: *the, they, them, thou, thee, thy, this, that, these*. This voicing may well have occurred by Chaucer's time.

(7) ME *–ng–* [–ŋg–] > [–ŋ–], as in *tongue, thing*. (Cf. the loss of [–b] in *lamb*, even though the [–d] in *hand* was not lost.)

(8) [–x–] was lost in words like *bough, bought*; it was also lost in words like *light, right, knight*, with compensatory lengthening of preceding [ɪ] to [iː], later [əɪ]. (In *laugh* and *enough* the [x] was not entirely lost, but was modified to [f]. The same sound in *trough* became either [θ] or [f]. Even in ME, the pronunciation of these words may have varied.) The spelling *gh* in *delight* is not historical (< ME *delīte*) but was added by analogy with *light*.

OTHER DEVELOPMENTS OF IMPORTANCE TO PRESENT-DAY ENGLISH

1. ME *ǭ* in *hǭt* and *gǭn* did not develop regularly into present-day [o], but shortened to [ɔ] or [ɑ], with some dialectal variation.

2. ME *ū* > MnE [u]   before labial consonants, *stoop* (vb.), *room, tomb* (respelled).

3. ME *–ǭr* > MnE [ɔɚ], *born, forlorn, sore, horse*.

4. ME *–ọ̄r* > MnE
$$\begin{cases} [\text{ʊɚ}], & boor, moor, poor \\ [\text{oɚ}], & door, floor, swore \end{cases}$$

5. ME *ū* before r + consonant > MnE [ɔ],   *court, source, course*.

6. ME $\begin{cases} -\bar{a}r- \\ -air- \end{cases}$ > MnE [ɛɚ] $\begin{cases} hare, fare, glare \\ fair, air, lair \end{cases}$

7. ME *ę̄r*   > MnE [ɪɚ],   *here, hear, deer, dear*

8. ME *–ẹ̄r–*   > MnE
$$\begin{cases} [\text{ɛɚ}], & wear, bear, tear \\ [\text{ɪɚ}], & ear, spear, fear \end{cases}$$

Regular Stressed Vowel and Diphthong Changes

OE Spelling	OE Sound	ME Spelling	ME Sound	EMnE Sound	MnE Sound	Examples (No distinction made here between EMnE and MnE)
ī ȳ	[iː] [yː]	ī, ȳ	[iː]	[əɪ]	[aɪ]	OE rīdan > ME ride(n) > MnE ride fȳr > fȳr > fire
ĭ y̆	[ɪ] [ʏ]	ĭ, y̆	[ɪ]	[ɪ]	[ɪ]	drincan > drinke(n) > drink fyllan > fille(n) > fill
ē ēo	[eː] [eːo]	ẹ̄, ẹẹ	[eː]	[iː]	[i]	fēt > fẹẹt > feet dēop > dẹẹp > deep ⎰MnE –ee–⎱ þēof > thẹ̄f > thief ⎱MnE –ie–⎰ < ME ẹ̄
ĕ ĕo	[ɛ] [ɛo]	ĕ	[ɛ]	[ɛ]	[ɛ]	helpan > helpe(n) > help heofon > heven > heaven
ǣ	[æː]	SE Midland (Chaucer) ẹ̄, ẹẹ [ɛː] → [ɛː]	[ɛː]	[e]	grēat > grẹ̄t > great (cf. yea, break, steak, drain)
ēa	[æːə]	→ [eː]	[iː]	[i]		clǣne > clẹẹne > clean (MnE –ea– <ME ẹ̄) strēam > strẹ̄me > stream SE (Kent, Essex) = stand. development
æ̆ ĕa	[æ] [æə]	ă	[ɑ]	[æ]	[æ]	þæt > that > that healf > half > half
ū	[uː]	ū, ou ow	[uː]	[əʊ]	[aʊ]	hūs > hous > house
ŭ	[ʊ]	ŭ, ŏ	[ʊ]	[ʊ,] ʌ	[ʊ, ʌ]	ful > full > full sunu > sone > son under > under > under
				blood [ʊ] ʌ	[ʌ]	blōd > blǒd > blood
ō	[oː]	ō, oo	[oː]	→ [ʊ]	[ʊ]	gōda > gǒod > good
			[uː] →	[u]		fōda > fōde > food
ŏ	[ɔ]	ŏ	[ɔ]	[ɔ]	[ɔ, ɑ]	oxa > oxe > ox (esp. in USA)
ā	[ɑː]	ǭ, oo	[ɔː]	[oː]	[o]	stān > stǫǫn > stone
ă	[ɑ]	ă	[ɑ]	[æ]	[æ]	crabba > crabbe > crab
		ā, aa ei, ai ey, ay	[ɑː] [æɪ]	[ɛː]	[e]	(OE nama >) nāme > name (OE twegen >) twein > twain (OE dæg >) day > day
		ǫu, ǫw	[ɔʊ]	[oː]	[o]	(OE grōwan >) grǫwe(n) > grow (OE blāwan >) blǫwe(n) > blow (OE boga [bɔɣɑ] >) bǫwe > bow
		au, aw	[ɑʊ]	[ɔː]	[ɔ]	(OE clāwu >) clawe > claw (OE tāht >) taughte > taught (OE dragan >) drawe(n) > draw
		ęu ęw iu iw, u	[ɛʊ] [iʊ]	[iʊ]	[u, ju]	(OE dēaw >) dęwe > dew (OE lǣwed >) lęwed > lewd (OE stīweard >) stęward > steward (OE brēowan >) bręwe(n) > brew vertu (OF) > virtue
		oi, oy	[ɔɪ]	[əɪ]	[ɔɪ]	boy, soil, toil, annoy (esp. Fr. words)

Part Two

English Texts, Transcriptions, Translations, and Exercises

THE OLD ENGLISH PERIOD[1]

The Prodigal Son

(*Luke* 15: 11–32)

TEXT

Hē cwæð. sōðlīċe sum man hæfde twegen suna.
þā cwæð sē yldra [=gingra?] tō his fæder;
Fæder. syle mē mīnne dǣl mīnre ǣhte þe mē
tō ge-byreþ. þā dǣlde hē him his ǣhte;

5 Ðā æfter fēawa dagum ealle his þing gegade-
rude sē gingra sunu. and fērde wrǣclīċe on
feorlen rīċe. and for-spilde þār his ǣhta lybbende
on his gǣlsan; Ðā hē hig hæfde ealle āmyrrede
þā wearð myċel hunger on þām rīċe and hē

10 wearð wǣdla; þā fērde hē and folgude ānum
burhsittendan men þæs rīċes. ðā sende hē hine
tō his tūne þæt hē hēolde his swȳn; Ðā ge-
wilnode hē his wambe gefyllan of þām bīen-
coddun þe ðā swȳn ǣton. and him man ne sealde;

15 Þā beþōhte hē hine and cwæð; Ēalā hū fela
ȳrðlinga on mīnes fæder hūse hlāf ġenōhne
habbað and iċ hēr on hungre forwurðe; Iċ
ārīse. and iċ fare tō mīnum fæder. and iċ seċge
him; Ēalā fæder iċ syngode on heofenas. and

20 beforan þē. nū iċ neom wyrðe þæt iċ bēo þīn
sunu nemned. dō mē swā ānne of þīnum ȳrð-
lingum;

and hē ārās þā and cōm tō his fæder. and þā
gȳt þā hē wæs feorr his fæder hē hine geseah

25 and wearð mid mild-heortnesse āstyrod and
agēn hine arn and hine beclypte and cyste hine;
Ðā cwæð his sunu; Fæder. iċ syngode on heofon.
and beforan ðē. nū iċ ne eom wyrþe þæt iċ þīn
sunu bēo genemned;

30 Ðā cwæþ sē fæder tō his þēowum; Bringað
raðe þæne sēlestan gegyrelan and scrȳdað hine
and syllað him hring on his hand. and gescȳ tō
his fōtum. and bringað ān fætt styriċ and of-
slēað and utun etan and gewist-fullian. for-þām

35 þes mīn sunu wæs dēad and hē ge-edcucude. hē
for-wearð and hē is gemēt; Ðā ongunnon hig
gewist-lǣcan[.]

TRANSCRIPTION

[heː kwæθ soːðliːče sʊm man hævdɛ twejen sʊna
θaː kwæθ seː ʏldra (jɪŋgra) toː hɪs fæder fæder
sʏlɛ meː miːnːɛ dæil miːnrɛ æɪxtɛ θɛ meː toː
jɛbʏrɛθ θaː dæːldɛ heː hɪm hɪs æɪxtɛ

θaː æfter fæɪawa daɣʊm æːliɛ hɪs θɪŋ jɛgadɛ- 5
rʊdɛ seː jɪŋgra sʊnʊ and feɪrdɛ wræːkliːčɛ ɔn
feorlen riːčɛ and fɔrspɪldɛ θaɪr hɪs æɪxta lʏbɪendɛ
ɔn hɪs gæɪlzan θaː heː hɪj hævdɛ æːliɛ aɪmʏrɪedɛ
θaː wæːrθ mɪčɛl hʊŋger ɔn θaɪm riːčɛ and heː
wæːrθ wæːdla θaː feɪrdɛ heː and fɔlɣʊdɛ aɪnʊm 10
bʊrxsɪtɪendan men θæs riːčɛs θaː sɛndɛ heː hɪnɛ
toː hɪs tuɪnɛ θæt heː heɪoldɛ hɪs swyɪn θaː
jewɪlnɔdɛ heː hɪs wambɛ jɛfʏlɪan ɔf θaɪm
biɪankɔdɪʊn θɛ θaː swyɪn æɪtɔn and hɪm man
nɛ sæːldɛ 15

θaː beθoɪxtɛ heː hɪnɛ and kwæθ æːlaɪ huɪ fɛla
yɪrðlɪŋga ɔn miːnɛs fæder huɪzɛ hlaɪf jenoɪxnɛ
habɪaθ and ɪč heɪr ɔn hʊŋgrɛ fɔrwʊrðɛ ɪč aɪriɪzɛ
and ɪč farɛ toː miːnʊm fæder and ɪč sejɛ hɪm
æːlaɪ fæder ɪč sʏŋgɔdɛ ɔn heovɛnas and befɔran 20
θeː nuɪ ɪč neom wʏrðɛ θæt ɪč beɪo θiɪn sʊnʊ
nɛmnɛd doɪ meː swaɪ aɪnɪɛ ɔf θiɪnʊm yɪrðlɪŋgʊm

and heː aɪraɪs θaː and koɪm toː hɪs fæder and
θaː jyɪt θaː heː wæs feor hɪs fæder heː hʏnɛ
jesæəx and wæːrθ mɪd mɪldheortnessɛ aɪstʏrɔd 25
and ajeɪn hɪnɛ arn and hɪnɛ beklʏptɛ and kʏstɛ
hɪnɛ θaː kwæθ hɪs sʊnʊ fæder ɪč sʏŋgʊdɛ ɔn
heovɔn and befɔran θeː nuɪ ɪč nɛ eom wʏrðɛ θæt
ɪč θiɪn sʊnʊ beɪo jɛnɛmnɛd

θaː kwæθ seː fæder toː hɪs θeɪowʊm brɪŋgaθ 30
raðɛ θænɛ seɪlestan jejʏrɛlan and šryɪdaθ hɪnɛ
and sʏlɪaθ hɪm hrɪŋg ɔn hɪs hand and ješyɪ toː
hɪs foɪtʊm and brɪŋgaθ aɪn fæɪt stʏrič and
ɔfslæɪaθ and ʊtʊn etan and jewɪstfʊlɪɪan fɔrðaɪm
θɛs miːn sʊnʊ wæs dæɪad and heː jɛɛdkʊkʊdɛ 35
heː fɔrwæːrθ and heː ɪs jɛmeɪt θaː ɔngʊnɪɔn
hɪj jewɪstlæɪkan

---

[1] This period lasted from 449 to 1100 A.D. The following
works were composed *c.* 700–1100. The texts are based on
manuscripts dating mainly from the tenth and eleventh
centuries.

36

TRANSLATION

He said: truly a certain man had two sons.
Then the younger said to his father: "Father,
give me my share of my goods that belongs to
me." Then he gave his goods to him.

5   Then after a few days the younger son
gathered all his belongings, and traveled abroad
to a distant land, and wasted his goods there,
living in his luxury. When he had squandered
it all, then a great famine came to that land,

10   and he became a poor man. Then he traveled
and followed a citizen of that land. Then he
sent him to his dwelling so that he might keep
his swine. Then he wanted to fill his stomach
with the beancods that the swine ate. And no

15   man gave (them) to him.

Then he thought to himself and said, "Alas,
how many servants have enough bread in my
father's house, and I perish here from hunger.
I will arise, and I will go to my father, and I

20   will say to him, "Alas, father, I have sinned
against heaven and before you. Now I am not
worthy to be named your son. Treat me as one
of your servants!"

And he arose then and went to his father.

25   And when he was yet far off, his father (he)
saw him, and was stirred with pity, and ran
toward him, and embraced him and kissed him.
Then his son said, "Father, I have sinned against
heaven and before you. Now I am not worthy

30   to be named your son."

Then the father said to his servants, "Bring
quickly the best robe and clothe him. And give
him a ring for his hand and shoes for his feet.
And bring a fatted steer and slay (it). And let

35   us eat and be joyful. For this my son was dead,
and he came to life. He perished, and he is
alive." Then they began to feast.

EXERCISES

1. What letters occur in OE which do not occur in MnE?

2. What MnE letters do not occur in OE?

3. Is there a pattern in the use of the OE letters "thorn" (þ, or Þ when capitalized) and "eth," or "crossed d" (ð, or Ð when capitalized)?

4. Compare the word order in the OE passage with the word order in the MnE translation. In what specific ways does OE word order apparently differ from MnE word order?

5. Does it take more or fewer words to translate an OE sentence into MnE? Find several sentences to support your conclusion and try to account for the difference.

6. By referring to the phonetic transcription, examine the distribution of voiced and voiceless *th* sounds ([ð] and [θ], respectively), voiced [v] and voiceless [f], and voiced [z] and voiceless [s], and see what rules for pronunciation you can make.

7. What frequently occurring vowel sound in MnE does not occur as a simple vowel at all in OE?

8. What really distinctive sounds occur in OE, in comparison to the sounds of MnE?

9. OE has long vowels as well as long consonants. This means that the sounds are articulated longer than if they were short. Do we speak of "long vowels" in MnE? Does MnE have long consonants?

10. List a dozen or more OE words (excluding short words like pronouns and conjunctions) beside MnE equivalents which resemble them, and see whether OE or MnE words tend to have more syllables.

11. How many reasons can you think of to account for this difference?

12. Compare the stress patterns of these OE words and their modern equivalents. (First, see p. 16 for OE stress patterns.) See if you can make an additional generalization or two about the difference between the pronunciation of OE and MnE prose.

13. MnE prose (no less than verse) frequently falls into an iambic pattern. Does OE prose seem to fall into this pattern?

TEXT CONTINUED

Sōðlīçe his yldra sunu wæs on æcere and hē
cōm. and þā hē þām hūse genēalǣhte hē ge-hȳrde
40 þæne swēg and þæt weryd. Þā clypode hē ānne
þēow and axode hine hwæt þæt wǣre; Ðā cwæð
hē þīn brōðor cōm. and þīn fæder of-slōh ān
fǣt çelf for-þām þe hē hine hālne on-fēng; Ðā
bealh hē hine and nolde ingān; þā ēode his fæder
45 ūt and ongan hine biddan;

Ðā cwæþ hē his fæder andswarigende; Efne
swā fela gēara iç þē þēowude and iç nǣfre þīn
bebod ne forgȳmde. and ne sealdest þū mē nǣfre
ān tiççen þæt iç mid mīnum frēondum gewist-
50 fullude; Ac syððan þes þīn sunu cōm. þe his
spēde mid myltystrum āmyrde. þū ofslōge him
fǣtt çelf; Ðā cwæþ hē sunu. þū eart symle mid
mē. and ealle mīne þing synt þīne[.] þe ge-byrede
gewist-fullian and geblissian for-þām þes þīn
55 brōðor wæs dēad and hē ge-edcucede hē for-
wearð and hē is gemēt. . . .

TRANSCRIPTION CONTINUED

soːðliːč̌e hɪs ʏldrɑ sʊnʊ wæs ɔn ækɛrɛ and
heː koːm ɑnd θɑː heː θɑːm huːze jɛnæːəlæːxtɛ heː
hyːrdɛ θæne sweːj ɑnd θæt wɛrʏd θɑː klʏpɔdɛ 40
heː ɑːnːɛ θeːow ɑnd ɑksɔdɛ hɪnɛ hwæt θæt
wæːrɛ θɑː kwæθ heː θiːn broːðɔr koːm and θiːn
fædɛr ɔfsloːx ɑːn fæːt č̌elf fɔrðɑːm θɛ heː hɪnɛ
hɑːlnɛ ɔnfeːŋg θɑː bæəlx heː hɪnɛ ɑnd nɔldɛ
ɪŋgɑːn θɑː eːodɛ hɪs fædɛr uːt ɑnd ɔŋgɑn hɪnɛ 45
bɪdːɑn

θɑː kwæθ heː hɪs fædɛr ɑndswɑrɪjɛndɛ ɛvnɛ
swɑː fɛlɑ jæərɑ ɪč̌ θeː θeːowʊdɛ ɑnd ɪč̌ næːvrɛ
θiːn bebɔd nɛ fɔrjyːmdɛ ɑnd nɛ sæəldɛst θuː
meː næːvrɛ ɑːn tɪč̌ːɛn θæt ɪč̌ mɪd miːnʊm 50
freːondʊm jɛwɪstfʊlːʊdɛ ɑk sʏθɑːn θɛs θiːn sʊnʊ
koːm θɛ hɪs speːdɛ mɪd mʏltʏstrʊm ɑːmʏrdɛ
θuː ɔfsloːɣɛ hɪm fæːt č̌elf θɑː kwæθ heː sʊnʊ θuː
æərt sʏmlɛ mɪd meː ɑnd æəlːɛ miːnɛ θɪŋg sʏnt
θiːnɛ θeː jɛbʏrɛdɛ jɛwɪstfʊlːɑn ɑnd jɛblɪsːɑn 55
fɔrðɑːm θɛs θiːn broːðɔr wæs dæːəd ɑnd heː
jɛədkʊkɛdɛ heː fɔrwæərθ ɑnd heː ɪs jɛmeːt]

TRANSLATION CONTINUED

Truly his elder son was in the field, and he came. And when he neared the house he heard
40 the noise and the company. Then he spoke to a servant and asked him what that was. Then he said, "Your brother came. And your father slew a fatted calf since he received him healthy." Then he became angry and would not go in.
45 Then his father came out and began to entreat him.

Then he said to his father, answering (him), "Even as many years I served you, and I never neglected your commandment. And you never
50 gave me a kid so that I feasted with my friends. But when this your son came, who squandered his riches on harlots, you slew him a fatted calf." Then he said, "Son, you are always with me, and all my things are yours. It is fitting
55 for you to feast and be joyful, for this your brother was dead and he came to life. He perished and he is alive."

The Lord's Prayer

(*Matthew* 6: 9–13)

TEXT

Fæder ūre
þū þe eart on heofonum,
Sī þīn nama gehālgod.

4 Tōbecume þīn rīçe.
   Ġewurþe ðīn willa on eorðan swā swā on heofo-
   num.
   Ūrne ġedæghwāmlīc<u>an</u> hlāf syle ūs tō dæg.   *— Acc. ending*
   And forgyf ūs ūrne gyltas, swā swā wē forgyfað
   ūrum gyltendum.

8 And ne gelǣd þū ūs on costnunge,
   ac ālȳs ūs of yfele. Sōþlīçe.

TRANSCRIPTION

[fæder uɪrɛ
θuɪ θɛ æərt ɔn hɛovɔnʊm
siɪ θiɪn nɑmɑ jɛhɑɪlɣɔd
toɪbɛkʊmɛ θiɪn riɪčɛ   4
jɛworðɛ θiɪn wɪlɪɑ ɔn ɛorðɑn swɑɪ swɑɪ ɔn
   hɛovɔnʊm
uɪrnɛ jɛdæjhwɑɪmliɪkɑn hlɑɪf sylɛ uɪs toɪ dæj
ɑnd fɔrjyf uɪs uɪrnɛ gyltɑs swɑɪ swɑɪ weɪ fɔrjɣvɑθ
   uɪrʊm gyltɛndʊm
ɑnd nɛ jɛlæɪd θuɪ uɪs ɔn kɔstnʊŋgɛ   8
ɑk ɑɪlyɪs uɪs ɔf yvɛlɛ soɪðliɪčɛ]

like → ly
friendly → friend-like

gyltendum ── Dat. ending
│
part. ending.

EXERCISES

1. Examine this and the preceding passage for words which have survived into MnE, and make an equivalence list of long vowels for OE and MnE. Check the results with the vowel chart on p. 33. (Note: a given OE vowel sound does not always develop in the regular way into a single MnE sound.)

2. How is OE *ū* frequently respelled in MnE? OE *ǣ*?

3. Study the use of prepositions in the passage and see what differences and similarities you can find between OE and MnE usage. What three meanings does OE *on* have here? Notice the suppressed preposition in line 6 (involving a "double" or indirect object). Does MnE still have this sort of construction?

4. List all the forms of the personal and possessive pronouns as they appear in this and the preceding selection. (See also the *Deor* selection.) Are these pronouns inflected more fully in OE than in MnE? State specifically the differences between the OE and MnE inflections. Now look at the declensions of these pronouns in a standard OE grammar (e.g., Moore and Knott, *Elements*, pp. 32, 44, and *passim*).

5. When a final *–um* occurs in an OE noun, what case seems to be signified?

6. It is quite common for OE diphthongs to be monothongized later (i.e., simplified to a single vowel). How many examples can you find in the prayer?

7. One of the ways that the word *who* could be expressed in OE was by the use of a personal pronoun plus a relative pronoun. Find an example.

8. In MnE, words with hard *g* [g] in them are often of Scandinavian origin and were borrowed in the late OE or in the ME period. The OE equivalents of these words have [j] instead. Find an example with [j] instead of the [g] which the modern speaker

TRANSLATION

Our Father,
thou who art in heaven,
thy name be hallowed.
4   Thy kingdom come.
Thy will be on earth as in heaven.
Give to us our daily bread today.
And forgive us our guilts, as we are forgiving
      to our sinners.
8   And do not lead (thou) us into temptation,
but free us from evil. Truly.

might expect. Find examples in the preceding selection of [j] sounds which remain in the language today, respelled *y*. (There is also a good example near the beginning of the next selection.)

9. The hard *g* [g] of MnE also exists in OE. Find examples. Notice the combination *–ng*. How does the *g* in this combination sound different from the *g* in the MnE combination *–ng*?

10. One of the distinctive morphological and phonetic features of OE is the unstressed *ġe–* [jɛ–] prefix, subsequently lost altogether through the intermediate ME stage *i–* [ɪ–]. Find examples and pronounce them.

11. Find an example of the other OE *g* sound, [ɣ]. This sound, when the word it is in survives, may become ME *w* [w]. Find other examples in the preceding selection.

12. Besides *ġe–*, other OE unstressed prefixes are *be–* and *for–*. Find examples in the preceding selection.

EXERCISES CONTINUED

13. OE verbs may be either weak or strong. Weak verbs are verbs which form their preterit (past tense) by adding a dental stop (*d* or *t*) at or near the end, whereas strong verbs are verbs which form their preterit by changing the vowel in their root syllable. The three principal parts of the OE weak verb are the infinitive, preterit singular (first person, indicative), and past participle, whose endings, respectively, are

> *–(i)an* (*ġefremman* 'to perform');
> *–ede, –de, –te, –ode, –ude, –ade* (*ġefremede* 'I performed');[2]
> *–ed, –d, –t, –od, –ud, –ad* (*ġefremed* 'performed').

To put matters more simply, the preterit singular ending consists of a *–d–* or a *–t–*, plus *–e*, and the past participle has a final *–d* or *–t*. Find examples of weak preterit singulars and weak past participles.

14. The four principal parts of the OE strong verb are the infinitive, preterit singular (first person indicative), preterit plural, and past participle, whose characteristic endings, respectively, are *–an*, *–ø*, *–on*, *–en*, as in *rīdan* 'to ride', *rād*, *ridon*, *ġeriden*. Find examples of the preterit plural (notice that MnE does not distinguish between preterit singular and plural) and of the past participle. What prefix is associated with the past participle? (Note: this prefix is sometimes dropped; it also occurs sometimes as a verbal prefix in all of the principal parts.) Here is an instance of inflection at both ends of a word—an unusual occurrence in English.

15. Normally, OE verbs, whether weak or strong, are conjugated as follows in the present tense:

> sing.   1   *–e*
> 2   *–(e)st*
> 3   *–(e)þ*
> pl.   1–3   *–aþ*

Find examples of these forms.

---

[2] The weak preterit plural varies from the singular in that it changes its ending to *–on*, as in *ġefremedon* 'we performed'; however, since its stem is identical to that of the preterit singular (*ġefremed–*), and since its grammatical function is so similar to the preterit singular, the preterit plural of weak verbs does not constitute a separate principal part.

The Laborers in the Vineyard

(*Matthew* 20: 1–16)

TEXT

Sōþlīce heofona rīċe is gelīċ þām hīredes ealdre
þe on ærne mergen ūt ēode āhȳrian wyrhtan on
his wīngeard. Gewordenre gecwydrǣdene þām
wyrhtum [þæt] hē sealde ælcon ǣnne penig wiþ
⁵ his dæges worce, hē āsende hig on his wīngeard.
And þā hē ūt ēode embe underntīde, hē geseah
ōþre on strǣte īdele standan. Ðā cwæð hē, gā
gē on mīnne wīngeard, and iċ sylle ēow þæt riht
byþ; and hig þā fērdon. Eft hē ūt ēode embe þā
¹⁰ sixtan and [þā] nigoþan tīde, and dyde þām swā
gelīċe. Þā embe þā endlyftan tīde hē ūt ēode,
and funde ōþre standende; and þā sǣde hē,
Hwī stande gē hēr eallne dæg īdele? Þā cwǣdon
hig, For þām þe ūs nān mann ne hȳrode. Ðā
¹⁵ cwæð hē, And gā gē on mīnne wīngeard.

Sōþlīce þā hit wæs æfen geworden, þā sǣde
sē wīngeardes hlāford his gerēfan, Clypa þā
wyrhtan, and āgyf him heora mēde; āgynn fram
þām ȳtemestan oþ þone fyrmestan. Eornostlīċe
²⁰ þā ðā gecōmon þe embe þā endlyftan tīde cōmon,
þā onfēngon hig ælċ his pening. And þā þe þǣr
ǣrest cōmon wēndon þæt hig sceoldon māre
onfōn; þā onfēngon hig syndrige penegas. Ðā
ongunnon hig murcnian ongēn þone hīredes
²⁵ ealdor, and þus cwǣdon, Þās ȳtemestan worhton
āne tīde, and þū dydest hig gelīċe ūs þe bǣron
byrþena on þises dæges hǣtan. Ðā cwæð hē
andswardigende hyra ānum, Ēalā þū frēond, ne
dō iċ þe nǣnne tēonan; hū ne cōme þū tō mē tō
³⁰ wyrċeanne wið ānum penige; Nim þæt þīn is,
and gā; iċ wylle þysum ȳtemestan syllan eal
swā myċel swā þē. Oþþe ne mōt iċ dōn þæt iċ
wylle? hwæþer þe þīn ēage mānful is, for þām
þe iċ gōd eom? Swā bēoð þā fyrmestan ȳtemeste,
³⁵ and þā ȳtemestan fyrmeste; sōþlīce manega synt
geclypede, and fēawa gecorene.

TRANSCRIPTION

[soːðliːt͡ʃe hɛovɔna riːt͡ʃe ɪs jɛliːt͡ʃ θɑɪm hiːrɛdɛs
æːldre θe ɔn ærːne mɛrjɛn uːt eːode ɑːhyːrɪɑn
wyrxtan ɔn hɪs wiːnjæərd jewɔrdenre jekw-
yːdræːdene θɑɪm wyrxtom θæt heː sæːlde æːlkɔn
ǣːnɪe penɪj wɪθ hɪs dæjɛs wɔrke heː ɑɪsɛnde hɪj ⁵
ɔn hɪs wiːnjæərd and θɑɪ heː uːt eːode ɛmbe
ʊndɛrntiːde heː jesæːɔx ɔːðre ɔn stræːte iːdele
standan θɑɪ kwɔθ heː gɑɪ jeː ɔn miːnɪe wiːnjæərd
and ɪc sylɪe eːow θæt rɪxt byθ and hɪj θɑɪ feɪrdɔn
ɛft heː uːt eːode ɛmbe θɑɪ sɪkstan and θɑɪ ¹⁰
nɪɣɔðan tiːde and dyde θɑɪm swɑɪ jɛliːt͡ʃe θɑɪ
ɛmbe θɑɪ ɛndlyftan tiːde heː uːt eːode and
fʊnde ɔːðre standende and θɑɪ sæːde heː hwiː
stande jeː heːr æːlɪne dæj iːdele θɑɪ kwæːdɔn
hɪj fɔr θɑɪm θe uːs nɑɪn man ne hyːrɔde θɑɪ ¹⁵
kwæːθ heː and gɑɪ jeː ɔn miːnɪe wiːnjæərd

soːðliːt͡ʃe θɑɪ hɪt wæs æven jewɔrden θɑɪ sæːde
seː wiːnjæərdes hlɑɪvɔrd hɪs jereɪvan klypa θɑɪ
wyrxtan and ɑɪjyf hɪm hɛora meɪde ɑɪjyn fram
θɑɪm yːtemestan ɔθ θone fyrmestan ɛɔrnɔstliːt͡ʃe ²⁰
θɑɪ θɑɪ jekɔːmɔn θe ɛmbe θɑɪ ɛndlyftan tiːde
kɔːmɔn θɑɪ ɔnfeɪŋgɔn hɪj æːlt͡ʃ hɪs penɪŋg and
θɑɪ θe θæːr æːrɛst kɔːmɔn weɪndɔn θæt hɪj
ʃeoldɔn mɑɪre ɔnfoɪn θɑɪ ɔnfeɪŋgɔn hɪj syndrɪje
penɛɣas θɑɪ ɔngʊnɪɔn hɪj mʊrknɪan ɔnjeɪn θone ²⁵
hiːredes æːldɔr and θʊs kwæːdɔn θɑɪs yːtemestan
wɔrxtɔn ɑɪne tiːde and θuː dydɛst hɪj jɛliːt͡ʃe uːs
θe bæːrɔn byrðena ɔn θɪzes dæjes hætan θɑɪ
kwæːθ heː andswardijende hyra ɑɪnʊm æːɔlɑɪ
θuː freɪond ne doɪ ɪč θe næːnɪe teɪonan huɪ ne ³⁰
kɔɪme θuː toɪ meɪ toɪ wyrt͡ʃæːɔnɪe wɪθ ɑɪnʊm
penɪje nɪm θæt θiːn ɪs and gɑɪ ɪč wylɪe θyzʊm
yːtemestan sylɪan æːl swɑɪ myt͡ʃel swɑɪ θeɪ ɔðɪe
ne moɪt ɪč doɪn θæt ɪč wylɪe hwæːðer θe θiːn
æːɔje mɑɪnful ɪs fɔr θɑɪm θe ɪč goɪd ɛom swɑɪ ³⁵
beɪoθ θɑɪ fyrmestan yːtemeste and θɑɪ yːtemestan
fyrmeste soːðliːt͡ʃe manɛɣa synt jeklypede and
fæːawa jekɔrene]

TRANSLATION

Truly the kingdom of God is similar to the master of the household who went out in the early morning to hire workers for his vineyard. Having reached an agreement with the workers

5 that he would give each of them a penny for his day's work, he sent them to his vineyard. And when he went out about the third hour, he saw others standing idle in the street. Then he said, "Go to my vineyard, and I will give

10 you what is right"; and they went there. Afterwards he went out about the sixth and the ninth hour, and did likewise. Then about the eleventh hour he went out and found others standing; and then he said, "Why do you stand

15 here idle all day?" Then they said, "Because no one (has) hired us." Then he said, "And you go to my vineyard."

Truly when it was evening, then the lord of the vineyard said to his steward ["reeve"], "Call

20 the workers, and give them their wages; begin from the last to the first." Truly when those came who arrived about the eleventh hour, (then) each received his penny. And those that (had) come there first thought that they ought

25 to receive more; then they separately received pennies. Then they began to complain to the master of the household, and thus said, "Those last worked one hour, and you treated them like us, who bore the burden in the heat of the

30 day." Then he said, answering one of them, "Alas (you) friend, I do you no wrong; didn't you come to me to work for a penny? Take what is yours, and go; I will give to the last (entirely) as much as (I give) to you. Am I

35 not allowed to do what I want to? Or is your eye evil because I am good? So will the last be first, and the first last; truly many are called, and few chosen."

EXERCISES

1. Like MnE, OE has only a simple preterit, i.e., only one conjugated form to indicate a general past tense. Also like MnE, OE may use the auxiliaries *had* or *have* plus the preterit form to indicate a more remote past. OE differs from MnE, however, in that it sometimes omits the auxiliary when this sense of the preterit is intended. Find a couple of examples in the second paragraph.

2. Since OE is highly inflected, the infinitive ending is enough to indicate that the form is an infinitive. The word *to* is not associated with the infinitive in OE as it usually is in MnE. The third sentence is a good illustration of OE practice. How is the infinitive here best translated? See also the third sentence of the second paragraph, where the modal auxiliary *ought* (*sceoldon*) is used with the infinitive, and the sentence following where a plain infinitive is used.

3. As in MnE, OE verbs have no special tense to indicate futurity. Whereas both OE and MnE may use auxiliary verbs to indicate the future tense, OE is likely to use the simple present tense. Find an example or two of each method in this selection. (Notice that when a helping verb is used, it is accompanied by an infinitive.)

4. Find two examples of the OE present participle, which ends in *–ende*.

5. A peculiar verbal construction in OE is the gerund. It is preceded by the preposition *to* and ends in *–enne* (less frequently *–anne*, by confusion with infinitives). Find an example near the end of the selection. Notice that it is here (and frequently) best translated into MnE as an infinitive. (Originally, the gerund was the dative case—final *–e* is associated with the dative—of the infinitive declined as a verbal noun.)

6. The MnE singular possessive case in *–s* for nouns is clearly anticipated by the OE *–es* ending of the genitive case. List several examples.

7. One of the ways that the word *who* (or *that*) could be expressed in OE was by the use of the indeclinable relative pronoun *þe* by itself. Find several examples. (OE *þe* does not develop into MnE *that*.)

8. A common way of expressing a "when" clause followed by a "then" clause is to begin both clauses with *þā*. Find an example. (Note: the second *þā*, meaning 'then', is often omitted in the MnE construction.)

Bede's Ecclesiastical History
Cædmon's Hymn

TEXT

In ðeosse abbudissan mynstre wæs sum brōðor
syndriglīçe mid godcundre gife gemæred ⁊
geweorðad. Forþon hē gewunade gerisenlīçe lēoð
wyrçan, þā ðe tō æfestnisse ⁊ tō ārfæstnisse
5 belumpen, swā ðætte, swā hwæt swā hē of
godcundum stafum þurh bōceras geleornode,
þæt hē æfter medmiclum fæce in scopgereorde
mid þā mæstan swētnisse ⁊ inbryrdnisse ge-
glængde ⁊ in Engliscgereorde wel geworht
10 forþbrōhte. Ond for his lēoþsongum monigra
monna mōd oft tō worulde forhogdnisse ⁊ tō
geþēodnisse þæs heofonlīcan līfes onbærnde
wæron. Ond ēac swelçe monige ōþre æfter him
in Ongelþēode ongunnon æfeste lēoð wyrçan:
15 ac nænig hwæðre him þæt gelīçe dōn meahte.
Forþon hē nales from monnum ne þurh mon
gelæred wæs, þæt hē þone lēoðcræft leornade,
ac hē wæs godcundlīçe gefultumed ⁊ þurh Godes
gife þone songcræft onfēng. Ond hē forðon
20 næfre nōht lēasunge, ne īdles lēoþes wyrçan
meahte, ac efne þā ān þā ðe tō æfestnesse
belumpon, ⁊ his þā æfestan tungan gedeofanade
singan.

Wæs hē sē mon in weoruldhāde geseted oð
25 þā tīde þe hē wæs gelȳfdre ylde, ⁊ næfre nænig
lēoð geleornade. Ond hē forþon oft in gebēorscipe,
þonne þær wæs blisse intinga gedēmed, þæt hēo
ealle scalde þurh endebyrdnesse be hearpan
singan, þonne hē geseah þā hearpan him
30 nēalēçan, þonne ārās hē for forscome from
þæm symble ⁊ hām ēode tō his hūse. Þā hē
þæt þā sumre tīde dyde, þæt hē forlēt þæt hūs
þæs gebēorscipes, ⁊ ūt wæs gongende tō nēata
scipene, þāra heord him wæs þære neahte
35 beboden. Þā hē ðā þær in gelimplīçe tīde his
leomu on reste gesette ⁊ onslēpte, þā stōd him
sum mon æt þurh swefn ⁊ hine hālette ⁊ grētte
⁊ hine be his noman nemnde: Cedmon, sing mē
hwæthwugu. Þā ondswarede hē ⁊ cwæþ: Ne
40 con iç nōht singan; ⁊ iç forþon of þeossum
gebēorscipe ūtēode, ⁊ hider gewāt, forþon iç

TRANSCRIPTION

[ɪn θɛosɪɛ ɑbɪʊdɪsɪɑn mʏnstrɛ wæs sʊm broɪðɔr
sʏndrɪjliːčɛ mɪd gɔdkʊndrɛ jɪvɛ jɛmæɪrɛd ɔnd
jɛwɛorðɑd fɔrðɔn heɪ jɛwʊnɑdɛ jɛrɪzɛnliːčɛ
leɪoθ wʏrčɑn θɑɪ ðɛ toɪ æɪvɛstnɪsɪɛ ɔnd toɪ
ɑɪrvæstnɪsɪɛ bɛlʊmpɛn swɑɪ θætɪɛ swɑɪ hwæt 5
swɑɪ heɪ ɔf gɔdkʊndʊm stɑvʊm θʊrx boɪkɛrɑs
jɛlɛornɔdɛ θæt heɪ æftɛr mɛdmɪklʊm fækɛ ɪn
šɔpjɛrɛordɛ mɪd θɑɪ mæɪstɑn swɛɪtnɪsɪɛ ɔnd
ɪnbrʏrdnɪsɪɛ jɛglæŋdɛ ɔnd ɪn ɛŋglišjɛrɛordɛ
wɛl jɛwɔrxt fɔrθbroɪxtɛ ɔnd fɔr hɪs lɛɪoθsɔŋgʊm 10
mɔnɪjrɑ mɔnɑ moɪd ɔft toɪ wɔrʊldɛ fɔrhɔɣdnɪsɪɛ
ɔnd toɪ jɛθeɪodnɪsɪɛ θæs hɛovɔnliːkɑn liɪvɛs
ɔnbærndɛ wæɪrɔn ɔnd æɪɑk swɛlčɛ mɔnɪjɛ oɪðrɛ
æftɛr hɪm ɪn ɔŋgɛlθeɪodɛ ɔngʊnɪɔn æɪvɛstɛ
leɪoθ wʏrčɑn ɑk næɪnɪj hwæðrɛ hɪm θæt jɛliːčɛ 15
doɪn mæɑxtɛ fɔrðɔn heɪ nɑlɛs frɔm mɔnɪʊm nɛ
θʊrx mɔn jɛlæɪrɛd wæs θæt heɪ θɔnɛ leɪoθkræft
lɛornɑdɛ ɑk heɪ wæs gɔdkʊndliːčɛ jɛfʊltʊmɛd
ɔnd θʊrx gɔdɛs jɪvɛ θɔnɛ sɔŋgkræft ɔnfeɪŋg ɔnd
heɪ fɔrðɔn næɪvrɛ noɪxt læɪəzʊŋgɛ nɛ iɪdlɛs 20
leɪoðɛs wʏrčɑn mæɑxtɛ ɑk ɛvnɛ θɑɪ ɑɪn θɑɪ ðɛ
toɪ æɪvɛstnɪsɪɛ bɛlʊmpɔn ɔnd hɪs θɑɪ æɪvɛstɑn
tʊŋgɑn jɛdɛovɑnɑdɛ sɪŋgɑn

wæs heɪ seɪ mɔn ɪn wɛorʊldhɑɪdɛ jɛsɛtɛd
ɔθɪɑ tiɪdɛ θɛ heɪ wæs jɛlyɪvdrɛ ʏldɛ ɔnd næɪvrɛ 25
næɪnɪj leɪoθ jɛlɛornɑdɛ ɔnd heɪ fɔrðɔn ɔft ɪn
jɛbɛoršɪpɛ θɔnɪɛ θæɪr wæs blɪsɪɛ ɪntɪŋgɑ jɛ-
deɪmɛd θæt heɪo æɪlɪɛ šɑldɛ θʊrx ɛndɛbʏrdnɪsɪɛ
bɛ hæɪrpɑn sɪŋgɑn θɔnɪɛ heɪ jɛsæɑx θɑɪ hæɪrpɑn
hɪm næɪəleɪčɑn θɔnɪɛ ɑɪrɑɪs heɪ fɔr fɔršɔmɛ 30
frɔm θæɪm sʏmblɛ ɔnd hɑɪm eɪodɛ toɪ hɪs huɪzɛ
θɑɪ heɪ θæt θɑɪ sʊmrɛ tiɪdɛ dʏdɛ θæt heɪ fɔrleɪt
θæt huɪs θæs jɛbeɪoršɪpɛs ɔnd uɪt wæs gɔŋgɛndɛ
toɪ næɪətɑ šɪpɛnɛ θɑɪrɑ hɛord hɪm wæs θæɪrɛ
næɑxtɛ bɛbɔdɛn θɑɪ heɪ θɑɪ θæɪr ɪn jɛlɪmpliːčɛ 35
tiɪdɛ hɪs lɛomʊ ɔn rɛstɛ jɛsɛtɪɛ ɔnd ɔnsleɪptɛ θɑɪ
stoɪd hɪm sʊm mɔn æt θʊrx swɛvn ɔnd hɪnɛ
hɑɪlɛtɪɛ ɔnd greɪtɪɛ ɔnd hɪnɛ bɛ hɪs nɔmɑn
nɛmndɛ kɛdmɔn sɪŋg meɪ hwæthwɔɣʊ θɑɪ
ɔndswɑrɛdɛ heɪ ɔnd kwæθ nɛ kɔn ɪč noɪxt sɪŋgɑn 40
ɔnd ɪč fɔrðɔn ɔf θɛosɪʊm jɛbeɪoršɪpɛ uɪteɪodɛ

TRANSLATION

In the monastery of this abbess was a certain
brother especially made famous and honored
by holy gift. For he was accustomed to make
suitable songs that pertained to piety and to
5 virtue, so that whatever he learned through
scholarship of religious letters, he adorned (it)
after a short interval in the language of poetry
with the most sweetness and humility, and
brought it forth well wrought in the English
10 language. And because of his songs the minds
of many men were often kindled with contempt
for the world and to the association of the
heavenly life. And likewise many others after
him began to compose religious songs in Eng-
15 land; but none, however, could do that like
him. For he was not taught at all by men or by
anyone what he (had) learned of that poetic
skill, but he was divinely helped and received
the art of poetry through a gift of God. And
20 therefore he could never compose anything of
falsehood or of idle song, but only those (words)
alone which related to religion and (could) sing
those that befit his pious tongue.

He was (the one) established in the secular
25 world until the time that he was of infirmed age
and (had) never learned any songs. And because he often went to a feast, when it was
deemed a cause of joy there that they all in
turn should sing to the harp, whenever he saw
30 the harp come near him, (then) he arose from
the feast on account of shame and walked home
to his house. Then he did that at a certain time,
so that he went out from the house of the feast
and was walking to the stable of the cattle,
35 which herd was entrusted to him for the night.
When at a suitable time he placed his limbs
there to rest and slept, then a certain man
stood by him in a dream and saluted and greeted
him and called him by his name: "Cedmon,
40 sing something to me." Then he answered and
said: "I don't know how to sing anything; and

EXERCISES

1. The OE noun may be either strong or weak.[3]
The strong noun is the more common. Nouns are
also categorized as masculine, feminine, or neuter.
Probably the most common is the strong masculine
declension exemplified by *stān* 'stone':

Sing. nominative *stān*		Pl. nominative *stānas*	
genitive	*stānes*	genitive	*stāna*
dative	*stāne*	dative	*stānum*
accusative	*stān*	accusative	*stānas*

Find an example of each case in this and the preceding selection. Notice that prepositions sometimes
cause nouns to take the dative and sometimes the
accusative case.

2. The weak noun is also quite common, and is
declined like *oxa* 'ox':

Sing. nominative *oxa*		Pl. nominative *oxan*	
genitive	*oxan*	genitive	*oxena*
dative	*oxan*	dative	*oxum*
accusative	*oxan*	accusative	*oxan*

Notice the relative lack of distinction among case
endings. Find several examples in the selection and
note the case of each example. (Note: the only OE
noun in this category to survive into MnE is *oxen*,
although *brethren*, *children*, and *kine* switched to
this category by analogy.)

3. The strong neuter nouns are distinctive because
the nominative and accusative plural forms are
identical with the nominative and accusative singular forms. Thus they are called the "unchanged
plurals." Otherwise, these nouns are declined like
stān above. This type is exemplified by *lēoð* (3, 10),
by *weorc* (51), and by *word* (60). Can you think
of three MnE nouns with unchanged plurals?

fish   sheep
deer   moose

[3] A strong noun is one whose Germanic stem had ended in
a vowel, and a weak noun is one whose Germanic stem had
ended in a consonant. The reasons for the designations "weak"
and "strong" are unimportant, however; what is important
is to note the inflectional differences between the two classes
of OE nouns.

TEXT CONTINUED

nāht singan ne cūðe. Eft hē cwæð sē ðe wið
hine sprecende wæs: Hwæðre þū meaht singan.
þā cwæð hē: Hwæt sceal iç singan? Cwæð hē:

45 Sing mē frumsceaft. þā hē ðā þās andsware
onfēng, þā ongon hē sōna singan in herenesse
Godes Scyppendes þā fers **7** þā word þe hē
næfre gehȳrde, þǣre endebyrdnesse þis is:

Nū sculon herigean heofonrīçes weard,
50   meotodes meahte **7** his mōdgeþanc,
weorc wuldorfæder, swā hē wundra gehwæs,
ēçe Drihten, ōr onstealde.
hē ǣrest scēop eorðan bearnum
heofon tō hrōfe hālig scyppend;
55   þā middangeard monncynnes weard,
ēçe Drihten, æfter tēode
fīrum foldan, frēa ælmihtig.

þā ārās hē from þǣm slǣpe, **7** eal, þā þe hē
slǣpende song, fæste in gemynde hæfde. **7** þǣm
60   wordum sōna moniġ word in þæt ilce gemet
Gode wyrðes songes tōgeþēodde.

TRANSCRIPTION CONTINUED

ɔnd hɪdɛr jɛwɑːt fɔrðɔn ɪč nɑːxt sɪŋgɑn nɛ kuːðɛ
ɛft heː kwæθ seː θɛ wɪθ hɪnɛ sprɛkɛndɛ wæs
hwæðrɛ θuː mæɔxt sɪŋgɑn θɑː kwæθ heː hwæt
šæɔl ɪč sɪŋgɑn kwæθ heː sɪŋg meː frumšæɔft θɑː   45
heː θɑː θɑːs ɑndswɑrɛ ɔnfeːŋg θɑː ɔngɔn heː
sɔːnɑ sɪŋgɑn ɪn hɛrɛnɛsːɛ gɔdɛs šypːɛndɛs θɑː
fɛrs ɔnd θɑː wɔrd θɛ heː næːvrɛ jɛhyːrdɛ θæːrɛ
ɛndɛbyrdnɛsːɛ θɪs ɪs

nuː šʊlɔn hɛrɪjæɔn hɛɔvɔnriːčɛs wæɔrd   50
mɛɔtɔdɛs mæɔxtɛ ɔnd hɪs mɔːdjɛθɑŋk
wɛɔrk wʊldɔrfædɛr swɑː heː wʊndrɑ jɛhwæs
eːčɛ drɪxtɛn ɔːr ɔnstæɔldɛ
heː æːrɛst šeːɔp ɛɔrðɑn bæɔrnʊm
hɛɔvɔn tɔː hrɔːvɛ hɑːlɪj šypːɛnd   55
θɑː mɪdːɑnjæɔrd mɔnːkynːɛs wæɔrd
eːčɛ drɪxtɛn æftɛr teːɔdɛ
fiːrʊm fɔldɑn fræːɔ ælmɪxtɪj

θɑː ɑːrɑːs heː frɔm θæːm slæːpɛ ɔnd æɔl θɑː
θɛ heː slæːpɛndɛ sɔŋg fæstɛ ɪn jɛmyndɛ hævdɛ   60
ɔnd θæːm wɔrdʊm sɔːnɑ mɔnɪj wɔrd ɪn θæt
ɪlkɛ jɛmɛt gɔdɛ wyrðɛs sɔŋgɛs tɔːjɛðeːɔdːɛ]

EXERCISES CONTINUED

4. Find several examples of the strong noun dative
case (singular in –e, plural in –um) being used without an accompanying preposition and several examples of the dative case being used with a preposition.
Notice that since MnE no longer has a separate
dative case, the preposition has to be used more
often, although not necessarily with the still highly
inflected personal pronoun.

5. The OE adjective agrees with nouns in number,
gender, and case, although its endings may not
resemble those of the noun it modifies. There are
masculine, feminine, and neuter declensions, and
most adjectives may be declined in either a weak
or a strong declension, depending on the position
of the adjective in the sentence. The weak inflection

(usually –an) is used primarily after the definite
article sē 'the' or the demonstrative pronoun þēs
'this', or after a possessive pronoun. A good example
is to be found in line 12. The strong adjective is a
mixture of pronominal endings (–re, –ra, –ne) and
nominal endings (–es, –um). Note the several examples in the lines of poetry above.

6. Unlike MnE, OE has a highly declined definite
article sē, sēo, þæt 'the' (nominative masculine,
feminine, and neuter, respectively), which also serves
as the demonstrative pronoun meaning 'that'. Thus,
even if the OE noun were not declined, it would be
possible to tell its case by the form of the accompanying demonstrative. The neuter þæt survives in
Chaucer as that, the other forms having been reduced to the invariable form þe 'the'.

OE has another demonstrative for this: þēs, þēos,
þis—nominative masculine, feminine, and neuter,

TRANSLATION CONTINUED

therefore I went out from this feast and came here, since I don't know how to sing anything."

45 Again he said, the one who was speaking with him: "Nevertheless you could sing." Then he said: "What shall I sing?" He said: "Sing to me (about) the creation." When he (then) received this answer, then he began at once to sing in praise of God the Creator the verses

50 and the words that he (had) never heard, in which the sequence is this:

Now we should praise the Protector of Heaven, the might of the Creator and his thought, the works of the Father of Glory, just as he,

55 eternal Lord, created the beginning of each wonder.
He first created heaven as a roof for the sons of the earth, holy Creator; then the Protector of Mankind, the eternal Lord, afterwards created the earth,

60 the world for men, Ruler Almighty.

Then he arose from the sleep and held fast in his memory all that he sang (while) sleeping. And at once joined to those words, in the same measure, many words of the song worthy for

65 God.

respectively—also fully inflected, but used less frequently. The only form which survives in Chaucer is *this*, from the neuter form *þis*.

Note the following forms in the passage. (The advanced student should consult an OE grammar for the full declensions, e.g., Moore and Knott, *Elements*, pp. 29, 40.) For how many of them can you identify the case?

þā (4, 8, 47)	*þāra* (34)	*þeossum* (40)
þæt (7, 32)	*þǣre* (34, 48)	*þās* (45)
þæs (12)	*sē* (42)	*þis* (48)
þone (17)	*þǣm* (58)	
þǣm (31)		

7. By comparing the OE with the MnE translation, make a list of all the compounds you can find. Other colorful compounds occur in *The Prodigal Son* above. How important does compounding seem to be as a method of forming words in OE?

8. Reprinted below is the text of a Northumbrian version of *Cædmon's Hymn*. The advanced student may wish to compare it with the W. Saxon version above. (Taken from Elliott Van Kirk Dobbie, *The Manuscripts of Cædmon's Hymn and Bede's Death Song* [New York: Columbia Press, 1937], p. 13.)

Nu scylun hergan   hefaenricaes uard
metudæs maecti   end his modgidanc
uerc uuldurfadur   sue he uundra gihuaes
eci dryctin   or astelidæ
he aerist scop   aelda barnū
heben til hrofe   haleg scepen.
tha middungeard   moncynnæs uard
eci dryctin   æfter tiadæ
firum fold[v]   frea allmectig
primo cantauit caedmon istud carmen.

1 *hergan*] *herg*$\overset{a}{e}$*n*   4 *dryctin*] With *yc* altered from *in*
7 *middungeard*] With first *d* altered from *n*

Beowulf, 1–25

TEXT

Hwæt, wē Gār-dena   in gēardagum,
þēodcyninga   þrym gefrūnon,
hū ðā æþelingas   ellen fremedon!
Oft Scyld Scēfing   sceaþena þrēatum,
5   monegum mægþum   meodsetla oftēah,
egsode eorlas,   syððan ǣrest wearð
fēasceaft funden;   hē þæs frōfre gebād,
wēox under wolcnum   weorðmyndum þāh,
oð þæt him ǣghwylç   ymbsittendra
10   ofer hronrāde   hȳran scolde,
gomban gyldan;   þæt wæs gōd cyning!
Ðǣm eafera wæs   æfter cenned
geong in geardum,   þone God sende
folce tō frōfre;   fyrenðearfe ongeat,
15   þē hīe ǣr drugon   aldorlēase
lange hwīle;   him þæs Līffrēa,
wuldres Wealdend   woroldāre forgeaf,
Bēowulf wæs brēme   —blǣd wīde sprang—
Scyldes eafera   Scedelandum in.
20   Swā sceal geong guma   gōde gewyrçean,
fromum feohgiftum   on fæder bearme,
þæt hine on ylde   eft gewunigen
wilgesīþas,   þonne wig cume,
lēode gelǣsten;   lofdǣdum sceal
25   in mægþa gehwǣre   man geþeon.

TRANSCRIPTION

[hwæt weː gɑːrdɛna ɪn jæːərdɑɣʊm
θeːodkynɪŋɑ θrʏm jɛfruːnon
huː θɑː æðelɪŋɑs ɛllɛn frɛmɛdon
ɔft ʃyld ʃeːvɪŋ ʃæəðɛnɑ θræətʊm
mɔnɛɣʊm mæːjðʊm mɛodsɛtlɑ ɔftæːəx   5
ɛgsɔdɛ ɛorlɑs sʏθɑn æːrɛst wæərθ
fæːəʃæəft fʊndɛn heː θæs froːvrɛ jɛbɑːd
weːoks ʊndɛr wɔlknʊm wɛorθmʏndʊm θɑːx
ɔθæt hɪm æːjhwʏlʧ ʏmbsɪtɪɛndrɑ
ɔvɛr hrɔnrɑːdɛ hyɪrɑn ʃɔldɛ   10
gɔmbɑn jʏldɑn θæt wæs gɔːd kʏnɪŋ
θæːm æəvɛrɑ wæs æftɛr kɛnɪɛd
jɛoŋ ɪn jæːərdʊm θɔnɛ gɔd sɛndɛ
fɔlkɛ toː froːvrɛ fʏrɛnθæərvɛ ɔnjæət
θeː hiːə æːr drʊɣon ɑldɔrlæːəzɛ   15
lɑŋɛ hwiːlɛ hɪm θæs liːfiːræːə
wʊldrɛs wæəldɛnd wɔroldɑːrɛ fɔrjæəf
beːowʊlf wæs breːm blæːd wiːdɛ sprɑŋg
ʃʏldɛs æəvɛrɑ ʃɛdɛlɑndʊm ɪn
swɑː ʃæːəl jɛoŋ gʊmɑ gɔːdə jɛwʏrʧæən   20
frɔmʊm fɛoxjɪftʊm ɔn fædɛr bæərmɛ
θæt hɪnɛ ɔn ʏldɛ ɛft jɛwʊnɪjɛn
wɪljɛziːðɑs θɔnɪɛ wiːj kʊmɛ
leːodɛ jɛlæːɪstɛn lɔfdæːɪdʊm ʃæːəl
ɪn mæːjðɑ jɛhwæːɪrɛ mɑn jɛθɛon]   25

TRANSLATION

Lo, we have heard of the glory of the people-kings of the spear-Danes in days of yore, how the nobles performed deeds of valor! Oft Scyld Scefing tore away the meadhouses from the
5 troops of the enemies, from many tribes, terrified the warriors, since he was first found poor; for that he experienced solace, prospered under the heavens, thrived in honors, until each of the neighboring peoples over the ocean ["whale
10 road"] had to listen to him, (had) to pay him tribute; he was a good king! Afterwards a son was born to him, young in the courtyard, whom God sent to the people for help; (God) saw (the) dire distress that they formerly (had)
15 suffered leaderless for a long while; for that the Lord of Life, the Ruler of Heaven, granted to him worldly honor, Beowulf was renowned— (his) glory spread far and wide—the son of Scyld in Danish lands. (Just) so should a young
20 man act with liberality, by splendid gifts of property in his father's possession, so that dear companions should stand by him afterwards in (his) old age, whenever war comes, people serve him; by praiseworthy deeds must one prosper
25 in each of the tribes.

EXERCISES

1. After reviewing the basic rules of stress on p. 16, and assuming that every syllable has either heavy stress or light stress, scan a dozen or so lines and see if you can determine any metrical principles holding the lines together.

2. In connection with the first exercise, read the lines aloud, stressing the alliterating sounds more heavily than the others, remembering that in OE verse any two vowels are considered to alliterate. How does reading make the lines sound different from the reading in the first exercise?

3. Now assume that each line has four heavy stresses, and each half-line two. Using alliteration as a guide for determining which syllables receive heavy stress, scan the lines again. This should give you some notion of OE metrics, although the details are not and perhaps never will be settled.

4. Does there seem to be a typical alliterative pattern? How many alliterating sounds are normally in a line?

5. Do the different lines seem to have an equal number of syllables? How does this compare with modern practice?

6. Reading the lines aloud again, try rapping a table top in time with the heavy stress beats. Does an equal amount of time seem to lapse between the heavy beats? Is there an equal number of unstressed syllables between heavy stresses? Is this the same as modern practice?

7. Do the separate lines seem to be self-contained syntactic units? Do the lines seem to fall into pairs syntactically? Is there any rhyme?

8. Modern practice divides OE poetic lines into half-lines. Can you discover a reason for this metrically? Syntactically?

9. Find two initial consonant clusters and one final consonant cluster that do not occur in MnE. Can you find other examples in other selections?

10. Can you determine the extent, if any, to which the word order here appears different from that of the preceding prose selections? In what ways does word order here seem different from that of modern verse? What sorts of syntactical patterns can an OE poet make that a modern one cannot? Why?

11. The word which becomes MnE *shall* occurs three times in the passage (10, 20, and 24). What is the basic meaning of the word, and how does its meaning differ from its MnE meaning?

3RD person - order - obligation

Deor

TEXT

Ƿēlund him be ƿurman   ƿræces cunnade,
ānhȳdiȝ eorl,   earfoþa drēaȝ,
hæfde him tō ȝesīþþe   sorȝe 7 lonȝaþ,
ƿinterçealde ƿræce,   ƿēan oft onfond
5   siþþan hine Nīðhād on   nēde leȝde,
sƿoncre seonobende,   on sȳllan monn.
    þæs oferēode; þisses sƿā mæȝ.

Beadohilde ne ƿæs   hyre brōþra dēaþ
on sefan sƿā sār   sƿā hyre sylfre þinȝ,
10   þæt hēo ȝearolīçe   onȝieten hæfde
þæt hēo ēacen ƿæs;   æfre ne meahte
þrīste ȝeþençan   hū ymb þæt sceolde.
    þæs oferēode; þisses sƿā mæȝ.

Ƿē þæt Mæðhilde   mōne ȝefruȝnon
15   ƿurdon ȝrundlēase   ȝēates frīȝe,
þæt hī sēo sorȝlufu   slæp ealle binōm.
    þæs oferēode; þisses sƿā mæȝ.

Ðēodrīç āhte   þrītiȝ ƿintra
Mæringa burȝ;   þæt ƿæs moneȝum cūþ.
20   þæs oferēode; þisses sƿā mæȝ.

Ƿē ȝēascodan   Eormanrīçes
ƿylfenne ȝeþōht;   āhte ƿīde folc
ȝotena rīçes;   þæt ƿæs ȝrim cyninȝ.
Sæt seçȝ moniȝ   sorȝum ȝebunden,
25   ƿēan on ƿēnan,   ƿȳscte ȝeneahhe
þæt þæs cynerīçes   ofercumen ƿære.
    þæs oferēode; þisses sƿā mæȝ.

Siteð sorȝçeariȝ,   sælum bidæled,
on sefan sƿeorceð,   sylfum þinceð
30   þæt sȳ endelēas   earfoða dæl,
mæȝ þonne ȝeþençan   þæt ȝeond þās ƿoruld
ƿītiȝ Dryhten   ƿendeþ ȝeneahhe,
eorle moneȝum   āre ȝescēapað,
ƿislīcne blæd,   sumum ƿēana dæl.

TRANSCRIPTION

[weːlʊnd hɪm be wʊrman wrækes kʊnːadɛ
aːnhyːdɪj ɛorl æərvɔða dræːəg
hævdɛ hɪm toː jesiːθːe sɔryɛ and lɔŋgaθ
wɪnterčæəldɛ wræke wæːən oft ɔnfɔnd
sɪθːan hɪne niːθhɑːd ɔn neːdɛ lɛjdɛ   5
swɔnkrɛ seonɔbendɛ ɔn syːlːan mɔn
    θæs ɔverɛːodɛ θɪsːɛs swaː mæj

bæədɔhɪldɛ nɛ wæs hyrɛ broːðra dæːəθ
ɔn sɛvan swaː saːr swaː hyrɛ sylvrɛ θɪŋg
θæt heːo jæərɔliːčɛ ɔnjɪəten hævdɛ   10
θæt heːo æːəken wæs æːvrɛ nɛ mæəxtɛ
θriːstɛ jeθɛnčan huː ymb θæt šeoldɛ
    θæs ɔverɛːodɛ θɪsːɛs swaː mæj

weː θæt mæːθɪldɛ moːnɛ jefrʊgnɔn
wʊrdɔn grʊndlæːəzɛ jæːətes friːjɛ   15
θæt hiː seːo sɔryʊvʊ slæːp æəlːɛ binɔːm
    θæs ɔverɛːodɛ θɪsːɛs swaː mæj

θeːodriːč aɪxtɛ θriːtɪj wɪntra
mæːrɪŋga bʊrg θæt wæs mɔnɛyʊm kuːθ
    θæs ɔverɛːodɛ θɪsːɛs swaː mæj   20

weː jɑːskodan ɛormanriːčes
wylvenɪɛ jeθoːxt aɪxtɛ wiːdɛ fɔlk
gɔtena riːčes θæt wæs grɪm kynɪŋg
sæt sɛǰ mɔnɪj sɔryʊm jebʊnden
wæːən ɔn weːnan wyːštɛ jɛnæəxɪɛ   25
θæt θæs kynɛriːčes ɔverkʊmen wæːrɛ
    θæs ɔverɛːodɛ θɪsːɛs swaː mæj

sɪteθ sɔryčæərɪj sæːlʊm bɪdæːled
ɔn sɛvan sweorkeθ sylvʊm θɪnkeθ
θæt syː ɛndɛlæːəs æːəvɔða dæːl   30
mæj θɔnɪɛ jeθɛnčan θæt jeond θaɪs wɔrʊld
wiːtɪj dryxten wendeθ jɛnæəxɪɛ
ɛorlɛ mɔnɛyʊm aɪrɛ ješæːəwɑθ
wɪsliːknɛ blæːd sʊmʊm wæːəna dæːl

TRANSLATION

Weland suffered exile among swords,
steadfast man, endured hardships,
had for companion sorrow and longing,
in winter exile, often suffered woe
5 after Niðhad laid fetters on him,
supple sinew-bonds, on (the) better man.
    That passed over; so can this.

Nor was to Beadohild the death of her brother
so sore in (her) heart as her own condition,
10 when she clearly had understood
that she was pregnant; nor could ever
confidently think how that should be so.
    That passed over; so can this.

We learned that Mæðhild's moans
15 became numberless (by means) of Geat's lady,
so that that distressing love robbed her of all
    sleep.
    That passed over; so can this.

Thodric held (for) thirty winters
(the) city of the Mæringas; that was known to
    many.
20   That passed over; so can this.

We have learned of Eormanric's
wolfish thought; held widely the folk
of the kingdom of the Goths; he was a grim king.
Many (a) man sat bound with sorrow,
25 in expectation of woe, often wished
that that kingdom were overcome.
    That passed over; so can this.

The sorrowful one sits, deprived of joy,
is sad in (his) spirit, thinks to himself
30 that (his) portion of hardship is endless,
is able to think that throughout this world
wise God often goes,
grants honor to many (a) man,
fame to certain (ones), a portion of woes to some.

EXERCISES

1. What symbols are used for *w* and *g* in this passage? (The symbol for *w* is called a "wen" — also, "wyn" or "wynn." The symbol for *g* is somewhat modified in EME and later written *y* or *g*. The modern *w* gained popularity later when it was used by Norman scribes; actually, it had been used in England in very early times in the form *uu*.)

2. In the latter half of the poem, find examples of a third person singular verb ending in –*eþ*. Also find there an instance of the future being indicated by an auxilary verb. (This auxilary originally denoted desire to do something and often has this meaning in OE texts, although it increasingly expresses simple futurity.)

3. In the refrain (cf. 31), what meaning does *mæʒ* (>MnE *may*) have? How does it differ from MnE usage?

4. What meaning does the *spā . . . spā* construction have in line 9? (*Spā*, or *swā*, >MnE *so*.)

5. What special meaning does *þæt* have in lines 16 and 35? (This usage is very common in OE and later in ME. Watch for other examples in other passages.)

6. Notice *sȳ*, the subjunctive form of the verb *to be*, in line 30. The subjunctive is used in OE much as it is used in Latin: 1) in a clause of purpose or result; 2) in a conditional clause; 3) in indirect discourse; and 4) in a command. What special subjunctive forms of the verb *to be* are used in MnE? Otherwise, to what extent is the subjunctive mood used in MnE? (OE verbs regularly have subjunctive forms, both present and preterit, the singular ending in –*e*, the plural ending in –*en*.)

7. The first line contains a reflexive pronoun (i.e., a personal pronoun used reflexively). Can you find another closeby? How are they to be translated into MnE? Compare the use of the reflexive pronoun in MnE.

8. Adverbs are commonly formed in OE by the use of the –*līçe* or –*e* suffix. Find examples in lines 10, 12, and 22, and look for others as you proceed

TRANSCRIPTION CONTINUED

35 þæt iç bi mē sylfum   secʒan þille,
    þæt iç hþīle þæs   Heodeninʒa scop,
    dryhtne dȳre;   mē þæs Dēor noma.
    Āhte iç fela þintra   folʒað tilne,
    holdne hlāford,   oþ þæt Heorrenda nū,
40 lēoðcræftiʒ monn,   londryht ʒeþah
    þæt mē eorla hlēo   ǣr ʒesealde.
       Þæs oferēode;   þisses sþā mæʒ.

θæt ɪč bɪ meː sylfʊm sɛjɑn wɪlːɛ   35
θæt ɪč hwiːlɛ wæs hɛodɛnɪŋgɑ šɔp
dryxtnɛ dyːrɛ meː wæs deːor nɔmɑ
ɑːxtɛ ɪč fɛlɑ wɪntrɑ fɔlɣɑθ tɪlnɛ
hɔldnɛ hlɑːvɔrd ɔθːæt hɛorːɛndɑ nuː
leːoθkræftɪj mɔn lɔndryxt jɛθɑx   40
θæt meː ɛorlɑ hleːo æːr jɛsæəldɛ
   θæs ɔvɛrɛodɛ θɪsːɛs swɑː mæj]

TRANSLATION CONTINUED

35 So that I will say about myself,
    that I was for a while the scop of the
      Heodeningas,
    dear to my Lord; my name was Deor.
    I had (an) excellent office for many winters,
    a gracious lord, until now Heorrenda,
40 a man skilled in song, received the landright
    that the protector of men once gave to me.
      That passed over; so can this.

EXERCISES CONTINUED

through the other passages. (OE *–līçe* > MnE *–ly*. When final *–e* is later lost, many adverbs become identical to the adjectives onto which the *–e* had originally been added; thus the lack of distinction in MnE between some adjectives and adverbs. Adverbs are also formed in German by adding *–e* to adjectives.)

9. By way of review, find examples of all the strong nominal cases given for *stān* on p. 45 above. (Notice that some nouns have *–e* where you would expect something else; there are several minor declensions which are not like *stān*.)

10. Examine, half-line by half-line, the technique used for the development of the ideas in the passage. Compare the way clauses and phrases are added to one another here with the similar procedure used in the *Beowulf* selection and in the hymn in the *Cædmon's Hymn* selection, and see what tentative conclusions you can come to about the nature of OE prosody.

The Anglo-Saxon Chronicle

TEXT

787. Hēr nōm Beorhtrīç cyning Offan dohtor
Ēadburge; ond on his dagum cuōmon ǣrest ·iii·
scipu, ond þā sē gerēfa þǣrtō rād, ond hīe
wolde drīfan tō þæs cyninges tūne þȳ hē nyste
hwæt hīe wǣron; ond hiene mon ofslōg; þæt
wǣron þā ǣrestan scipu Deniscra monna þe
Angel cynnes lond gesōhton·

895. Ond þā sōna æfter þǣm on ðȳs gēre fōr
sē here of Wīrhēale in on Norð Wēalas. forþǣm
hīe ðǣr sittan ne mehton; þæt wæs forðȳ þe
hīe wǣron benumene ægðer ge þæs çēapes, ge
þæs cornes, ðe hīe gehergod hæfdon; þā hīe ðā
eft ūt of Norð Wēalum wendon mid þǣre here-
hȳðe þe hīe ðǣr genumen hæfdon, þā fōron hīe
ofer Norðhymbra lond ond Ēast Engla, swā swā
sīo fird hīe gerǣcan ne mehte, oþþæt hīe cōmon
on Ēast Seaxna lond ēasteweard, on ān īgland
þæt is ūte on þǣre sǣ, þæt is Meresig hāten.
Ond þā sē here eft hāmweard wende. þe Exan-
ceaster beseten hæfde, þā hergodon hīe ūp on
Sūð Seaxum nēah Çisseçeastre, ond þā burgware
hīe geflīemdon, ond hira monig hund ofslōgon,
ond hira scipu sumu genāmon.

Ðā þȳ ylcan gēre onforan winter þā Deniscan
þe on Meresige sǣton. tugon hira scipu ūp on
Temese, ond þā ūp on Lȳgan; þæt wæs ymb
twā gēr þæs þe hīe hider ofer sǣ cōmon.

901. Hēr gefōr Ælfrēd Aþulfing, syx nihtum
ǣr ealra hāligra mæssan; Sē wæs cyning ofer
eall Ongelcyn būtan ðǣm dǣle þe under Dena
onwalde wæs, ond hē hēold þæt rīçe ōþrum
healfum lǣs þe ·xxx· wintra. Ond þā fēng
Ēadweard his sunu tō rīçe. . . .

1066. . . . And Harold eorl fēng tō Engla-
landes cynerīçe. swā swā sē cyng hit him geūðe.
And ēac men hine þǣr tō gecuron. And wæs
geblētsod tō cynge on twelftan mæsse dæg. And
þȳ ilcan gēare þe hē cyng wæs. hē fōr ūt mid
sciphere tōgēanes Willelme. . . . And þā hwīle
cōm Willelm eorl upp æt Hestingan on scē
Michaeles mæsse dæg. And Harold cōm norðan

TRANSCRIPTION

787. [heɪr noɪm bɛorxtriːč kʏnɪŋg ɔfɪan dɔxtɔr
æɪədburge ɔnd ɔn hɪs daɣʊm kʊoɪmɔn æɪrɛst
θreɪo šɪpʊ ɔnd θaɪ seɪ jɛreɪva θæɪrtoɪ raɪd ɔnd
hiːə wɔldɛ driːvan toɪ θæs kʏnɪŋgɛs tuɪnɛ θyɪ heɪ
nʏstɛ hwæt hiːə wæɪrɔn ɔnd hɪənɛ mɔn ɔfsloɪɣ
θæt wæɪrɔn θaɪ æɪrɛstan šɪpʊ dɛnɪšra mɔnɪa θɛ
angɛl kʏnɪɛs lɔnd jɛsoɪxtɔn

895. ɔnd θaɪ soɪna æftɛr θæɪm ɔn θyɪs jɛɪrɛ
foɪr seɪ hɛre ɔf wiːrhæɪələ ɪn ɔn nɔrθ wæɪalas
forðæɪm hiːə θæɪr sɪtɪan nɛ mɛxtɔn θæt wæs
forðyɪ θɛ hiːə wæɪrɔn bɛnʊmɛnɛ æjðɛr jɛ θæs
čæɪapɛs jɛ θæs kɔrnɛs θɛ hiːə jɛhɛrɣɔd hævdɔn
θaɪ hiːə θaɪ ɛft uɪt ɔf nɔrθ wæɪalʊm wɛndɔn mɪd
θæɪrɛ hɛrɛhyɪðɛ θɛ hiːə θæɪr jɛnʊmɛn hævdɔn
θaɪ foɪrɔn hiːə ɔver nɔrθhʏmbra lɔnd ɔnd æɪast
ɛŋgla swaɪ swaɪ siɪo fɪrd hiːə jɛræɪčan nɛ mɛxtɛ
ɔθæt hiːə koɪmɔn ɔn æɪast sæəksna lɔnd æɪastɛ-
wæərd ɔn aɪn iɪjland θæt ɪs uɪtɛ ɔn θæɪrɛ sæɪ
θæt ɪs mɛrɛsɪj haɪtɛn ɔnd θaɪ seɪ hɛre ɛft
haɪmwæərd wɛndɛ θɛ ɛksančæɪastɛr bɛsɛtɛn
hævdɛ θaɪ hɛrɣɔdɔn hiːə uɪp ɔn suɪθ sæəksʊm
næɪəx čɪsɪɛčæɪastre ɔnd θaɪ burgware hiːə jɛ-
fliːəmdɔn ɔnd hɪra mɔnɪj hʊnd ɔfsloɪɣɔn ɔnd
hɪra šɪpʊ sʊmʊ jɛnaɪmɔn

θaɪ θyɪ ʏlkan jɛɪrɛ ɔnforan wɪntɛr θaɪ dɛnɪšan
θɛ ɔn mɛrɛsɪjɛ sæɪtɔn tʊɣɔn hɪra šɪpʊ uɪp ɔn
tɛmɛzɛ ɔnd θaɪ uɪp ɔn lyɪgan θæt wæs ʏmb twaɪ
jɛɪr θæs θɛ hiːə hɪdɛr ɔver sæɪ koɪmɔn

901. heɪr jɛfoɪr ælvreɪd aðʊlfɪŋg sʏks nɪxtʊm
æɪr æɪlra haɪliɪjra mæɪsɪan seɪ wæs kʏnɪŋg ɔver
æɪl ɔŋgɛlkʏn buɪtan θæɪm dæɪlɛ θɛ ʊndɛr dɛna
ɔnwaldɛ wæs ɔnd heɪ hɛɪold θæt riɪčɛ oɪðrʊm
hæɪlvʊm læɪs θɛ θriːtɪj wɪntra ɔnd θaɪ feɪŋg
æɪdwæərd hɪs sʊnʊ toɪ riɪčɛ

1066. ɔnd harɔld ɛorl feɪŋg toɪ ɛŋglalandɛs
kʏnɛriɪčɛ swaɪ swaɪ seɪ kʏŋg hɪt hɪm jɛuɪðɛ ɔnd
æɪak mɛn hɪnɛ θæɪr toɪ jɛkʊrɔn ɔnd wæs jɛ-
blɛɪtsɔd toɪ kʏŋgɛ ɔn twɛlftan mæsɪɛ dæj ɔnd
θyɪ ɪlkan jæɪrɛ θɛ heɪ kʏŋg wæs heɪ foɪr uɪt
mɪd šɪphɛrɛ toɪjæɪanɛs wɪlɪɛlmɛ . . . . ɑnd θaɪ
hwiɪlɛ koɪm wɪlɪɛlm ɛorl ʊp æt hɛstɪŋgan ɔn

TRANSLATION

787. In this year King Beorhtric took (in marriage) Offa's daughter, Eadburge; and in his days came the first three ships, and then the reeve rode thereto, and wanted to conduct

5 them to the king's town before he knew who they were; and someone slew him; that was the first ships of Danish men who sought the land of the (race of the) Angels.

895. And then immediately afterwards in this

10 year the (Danish) army proceeded from the Wirral into North Wales, for they were not able to remain there; that was because they were robbed both of the cattle and of the grain that they had captured; when they afterwards went

15 out of North Wales with the booty that they had taken there, then they marched over Northumbria and East Anglia, so that the (British) army could not reach them until they came eastward into East Saxony, on an island that

20 is out in the sea, that is called Mersey. And when the (Danish) army that had besieged Exeter (afterwards) went homeward, (then) they ravaged inland to South Saxony near Chichester, and the inhabitants fled, and (they) slew many

25 hundreds of them and seized some of their ships.

In the same year before winter, the Danes who remained in Mersey brought their ships up into the Thames and then up the Lea; that was two years after (that) they (had) come

30 hither over the sea.

901. In this year Ælfred Athulfing died, six nights before the mass of All Saints' Day; he was king over all England except the portion that was under the rule of the Danes, and he

35 held the kingdom twenty-eight and a half years (i.e., "one and a half less than thirty winters"). And then Edward his son came to the throne. . . .

1066. . . . And earl Harold came to the throne of England just as the king (had) granted (it)

40 to him, and also men chose him (thereto). And (he) was blessed as king on the twelfth mass

EXERCISES

1. What generalizations can you make about the consistency of OE punctuation and capitalization? Under what circumstances is the period used?

2. Compare the syntax of this functional prose with the prose in previous selections. Explain and illustrate the differences.

3. What is the meaning of the following words? *sōna* (8), *dǣle* (30), *wið* (42), *sealdon* (47). To what extent has each word changed meaning?

4. Using words such as *Meresiġ* (18), *moniġ* (22), *hāliġra* (29), and *ġēare* (38) as evidence, what would you predict is the frequent development of OE palatal *g* (or *iġ*)? Considering *æġðer* (11), *īġland* (17), *dæġ* (37), and *twæġen* (43), determine the effect *g* has subsequently had on the preceding vowel. What has happened to the *g* itself in such instances?

5. What has become of palatal *ċ* in words like *ġerǣċan* (16) and *Ċiseċeastre* (21)?

6. Find words containing the consonant cluster *sc* and note the OE pronunciation. How has OE *sc* subsequently been respelled?

7. Pronounce the following OE words, paying particular attention to the sounds of the long vowels. Then pronounce the MnE equivalents of the words and determine how the OE vowels have been respelled and repronounced:

> *rād* (3), *swā* (15), *hāmweard* (19)
> *hē* (4)
> *drīfan* (4), *īġland* (17), *hwīle* (39)
> *tūne* (4), *ūt* (38)
> *sǣ* (18), *dǣle* (30)

8. Now check the vowel chart on p. 33 for each of these sounds. Notice that the subsequent development of OE *ō* is complex. Also notice how little the short vowels have changed pronunciation and spelling.

9. The presence of *ān* in line 17 reminds us how infrequently the word appears, and makes the fact occur to us that the similar form *a* isn't used at all in OE. Is the indefinite article needed in OE? In MnE? (The indefinite article *an* develops in the

TEXT CONTINUED

and him wið feaht ēar þan þe his here cōme eall.
And þǣr hē fēoll. And his twægen gebrōðra
Gyrð and Lēofwine. And Willelm þis land
45 geēode. and cōm tō Westmynstre. And Ealdrēd
arceƀ hine tō cynge gehālgode. and menn guldon
him gyld. and gīslas sealdon. and syððan heora
land bohtan. . . .

TRANSCRIPTION CONTINUED

saŋktɛ mɪkhɑɛlɛs mæsːɛ dæj ɑnd hɑrɔld koːm
nɔrðɑn ɑnd hɪm wɪθ fæəxt æːər θɑn θɛ hɪs hɛrɛ
koːmɛ æəl ɑnd θæːr heː feːol ɑnd hɪs twæjɛn
jɛbroːðrɑ ɡʏrθ ɑnd leːofwɪnɛ ɑnd wɪlːɛlm θɪs   45
lɑnd jɛeːodɛ ɑnd koːm toː wɛstmʏnstrɛ ɑnd
æəldreːd ɑrkɛbɪšɛp hɪnɛ toː kʏŋɡɛ jɛhɑːlyɔdɛ
ɑnd mɛn ɡʊldɔn hɪm ɡʏld ɑnd jiːzlɑs sæəldɔn
ɑnd sʏθːɑn heorɑ lɑnd bɔxtɑn]

TRANSLATION CONTINUED

day. And in the same year that he was king, he went out with the navy against William. . . . And meanwhile earl William came inland at
45 Hastings on St. Michaelmas Day. And Harold came north and fought against him before his whole army came. And there he fell, and his two brothers, Gyrth and Leofwine. And William conquered this land and came to Westminster,
50 and Archbishop Ealdred consecrated him as king, and men paid tribute to him and gave hostages and afterwards bought their land. . . .

EXERCISES CONTINUED

OE period from *ān* 'one', i.e., *an* is the unstressed form of *ān*. The word *a*, the unstressed form, in turn, of *an*, appears later when, in most cases, the −*n* is lost. Thus *an* appears in English before *a*, even though it is used much less than *a* in MnE. OE stressed *ān* regularly > ME *ǭn* > MnE *one*.)

10. Notice the phrase *Đā þȳ ylcan gēre* (24). The use of the strange form *þȳ* 'the' indicates the instrumental case, which denotes means or instrument. It is most obvious in the inflections of the demonstrative pronouns, appearing as *þȳ/þon/þē* and *þȳs/þisse/þis(se)re*. The instrumental also appears in the inflection of nouns, where it is identical to the dative endings. It is used, as here, in expressions of time (*þȳ ylcan mōnthe ond dæge* 'in the same month and day'), with comparatives (*sē eorl wæs þē blīþra* 'the earl was the happier'), and with nouns in the sense of the Latin ablative absolute (*ūp sprungenre sunne* 'the sun being sprung up'). For another example of this last use, see the *Laborers in the Vineyard* selection, line 3. (Examples given here are taken from Anderson and Williams, *Handbook*, p. 129.) The OE instrumental is preserved in the MnE pattern '*the* more *the* merrier' (in OE, *þȳ māre þȳ myrigre*). Find other uses of the instrumental case in this selection.

11. Notice the form *nyste* (4), a telescoping or blending of *ne wyste*, 'not'+'know'. This sort of assimilation of sounds is common in OE and ME. What causes it? To what extent does it occur in MnE? Give examples. Sometimes the OE demonstrative, otherwise almost entirely lost, is preserved because of assimilation, or "metanalysis": e.g., *the tother* < *þæt ōþer*; Atterbury < *æt þǣre byrig* ('at/in the town'):

Nash < { *æt þam æsce* / *at þen ashe* } the one who lives 'by the ash tree'.

Bede's Ecclesiastical History
The Conversion of Edward

TEXT

Þā sē cyning þā þās word gehȳrde, þā andswa-
rode hē him ond cwæð, þæt hē æghwæþer ge
wolde ge sceolde þām gelēafan onfōn þe hē
lǣrde. Cwæð hwæþere, þæt hē wolde mid his
5 frēondum ond mid his wytum gesprec ond
geþeaht habban, þæt gif hī mid hine þæt
geþafian woldan, þæt hī ealle ætsomme on līfes
willan Criste gehālgade wǣran. Þā dyde sē
cyning swā swā hē cwæð, ond sē bisceop þæt
10 geþafade....

    Þæs wordum ōþer cyninges wita ond ealdor-
mann geþafunge sealde, ond tō þǣre sprǣçe
fēng ond þus cwæð: þyslīç mē is gesewen, þū
cyning, þis andwearde līf manna on eorðan tō
15 wiðmetenesse þǣre tīde, þe ūs uncūð is, swylç
swā þū æt swǣsendum sitte mid þīnum ealdor-
mannum ond þegnum on wintertīde, ond sīe
fȳr onǣlæd ond þīn heall gewyrmed, ond hit
rīne ond snīwe ond styrme ūte; cume ān spearwa
20 ond hrædlīçe þæt hūs þurhflēo, cume þurh ōþre
duru in, þurh ōþre ūt gewīte. Hwæt hē on þā
tīd, þe hē inne bið, ne bið hrinen mid þȳ storme
þæs wintres; ac þæt bið ān ēagan bryhtm ond
þæt lǣsste fæc, ac hē sōna of wintra on þone
25 winter eft cymeð. Swā þonne þis monna līf tō
medmiclum fæce ætȳweð; hwæt þǣr foregange,
oððe hwæt þǣr æfterfylige, wē ne cunnun.
Forðon gif þēos lār ōwiht cūðlīcre ond gerisen-
līcre brenge, þæs weorþe is þæt wē þǣre fylgen.
30 Þeossum wordum gelīcum ōðre aldormen ond
ðæs cyninges geþeahteras sprǣcan....

    Ono hwæt hē þā wæs sē cyning openlīçe
ondettende þam biscope ond him eallum, þæt
hē wolde fæstlīçe þam dēofolgildum wiðsacan
35 ond Cristes gelēafan onfōn.

TRANSCRIPTION

[θɑː seː kʏnɪŋ θɑː θɑːs wɔrd jehyːrdə θɑː
ɑndswɑrɔdə heː hɪm ɔnd kwæθ θæt heː æːjhwæðer
jə wɔldə jə šeoldə θɑːm jəlæːəvɑn ɔnvoːn θe heː
læːrdə kwæθ hwæðerə θæt heː wɔldə mɪd hɪs
5 freiɔndum ɔnd hɪs wʏtum jesprek ɔnd jəθæəxt
hɑbiɑn θæt jɪf hiː mɪd hɪnə θæt jəθɑviɑn wɔldɑn
θæt hiː æəliː æt sɔmiː ɔn liːves wɪliɑn krɪstə
jehɑːlʏɑdə wæːrɑn θɑː dʏdə seː kʏnɪŋ swɑː swɑː
heː kwæθ ɔnd seː bɪšeop θæt jəθɑvɑdə

10 θæs wɔrdum oːðer kʏnɪŋges wɪtɑ ɔnd æəldɔr-
mɑn jəθɑvʊŋə sæəldə ɔnd toː θæːrə spræːčə
feɪŋ ɔnd θʊs kwæθ θʏsliːč meː ɪs jesewen θuː
kʏnɪŋ θɪs ɑndwæərdə liːf mɑniɑ ɔn eorðɑn toː
wɪθmetenesiː θæːrə tiːdə θe uːs ʊnkuːθ ɪs swʏlč
15 swɑː θuː æt swæːzendum sɪtiː mɪd θiːnum
æəldɔrmɑniʊm ɔnd θejnum ɔn wɪntertiːdə ɔnd
siiː fʏːr ɔnæːlæd ɔnd θiːn hæəl jewʏrmed ɔnd
hɪt riːnə ɔnd sniːwe ɔnd stʏrmə uːtə kʊmə
ɑːn spæərwɑ ɔnd hrædliːčə θæt huːs θʊrxfleiɔ
20 kʊmə θʊrx oːðrə dʊrʊ ɪn θʊrx oːðrə uːt jewiːtə
hwæt heː ɔn θɑː tiːd θe heː ɪniː bɪθ ne bɪθ hrɪnən
mɪd θʏː stɔrmə θæs wɪntrəs ɑk θæt bɪθ ɑːn
æəɣɑn brʏxtm ɔnd θæt læːsiːtə fæk ɑk heː soːnɑ
ɔf wɪntrɑ ɔn θɔne wɪnter ɛft kʏmeθ swɑː θɔniə
25 θɪs mɔniɑ liːf toː medmɪklʊm fækə ætʏːweθ
hwæt θæːr fɔregɑŋə ɔθiː hwæt θær æfterfʏlijə
weː ne kʊniʊn fɔrðɔn jɪf θeos lɑːr oːwɪxt
kuːðliːkrə ɔnd jeriːzenliːkrə breŋə θæs weorðə
ɪs θæt weː θæːrə fʏljen θeosiʊm wɔrdum jəliːkum
30 oːðrə ɑldɔrmɛn ɔnd θæs kʏnɪŋges jəθæəxterɑs
spræːkɑn

ɔno hwæt heː θɑː wæs seː kʏnɪŋ ɔpenliːčə
ɔndetiɛndə θɑm bɪšɔpə ɔnd hɪm æəliʊm θæt heː
wɔldə fæstliːčə θɑm deiɔvɔlgɪldum wɪθsɑkɑn
ɔnd krɪstɛs jəlæːəvɑn ɔnvoːn] 35

TRANSLATION

When the king heard these words, then he answered him and said that he (both) wanted to and was obligated to receive the faith that he [the bishop] taught. He said, however, that
5 he wished to have conversation with his friends and with his counsellors and have (their) advice, so that if they would consent to it with him they all would be consecrated together in Christ in the well of life. Then the king did as he said,
10 and the bishop consented to it.

After that another of the king's advisors and noblemen gave (his) consent to (his) words and took up the conversation and thus said: "Thus it seems to me, thou king, (that) this present life
15 of men on earth in comparison to the time that is unknown to us (is) just as if you were sitting at dinner with your noblemen and followers in the wintertime and a fire were kindled and your hall warmed and it rained and snowed and
20 stormed without; (and as if) a sparrow came and quickly flew through the house—came in through one door and went out through another. Lo, in the time that he is within he is not touched by the storm of winter; but that is a
25 twinkling of an eye and the least interval, and he passes at once from winter to winter again. So then this life of men appears as a limited interval: what goes before, or what follows after, we know not. Therefore if this doctrine brings
30 anything more clear and more fitting, it is appropriate that we follow it." With words similar to these, other noblemen and counsellors of the king spoke. . . .

Lo, then the king publicly confessed to the
35 bishop and to them all that he wished firmly to renounce devil-worship and receive the faith of Christ.

EXERCISES

1. This celebrated passage of OE, even though a translation from Latin, illustrates the great potential which English prose has. Notice the ease with which the translator handles some fairly complex English syntax. Compare in specific ways the style of this passage with the very different style of *The Prodigal Son*, which is also a fine piece of English translation.

2. Account for the distinctive verb forms in lines 16 ff. (*sitte, sīe, rīne, snīwe, styrme*, etc.).

3. How have the following words changed in meaning from OE times: *lǣrde* [<*lǣran*] (4), *uncūð* (15), *lār* (28), *aldormen* (30)? We still have the meaning denoted in *openlīçe* (32); do we still have the same meaning of *fast* as it is used in *fastlīçe*? We still have the word *uncouth*, but do we have *couth* (cf. line 28 and also Chaucer's "*kowthe* in sondry londes," *Gen. Prol.*, 14)?

4. What form might you expect in line 2 instead of *him*? (Cf. the related form in line 6.) The use of *him* shows that the accusative form is falling together with the dative, the dative providing the model form. What case is *mē* in line 13? *Ūs* in line 15? (Obviously, these are the forms that come down into MnE. For some reason the accusative case of the personal pronouns does not provide the model form as it does in the noun declensions. Older OE accusative *mec* and *ūsic* give way in late OE to *mē* and *ūs* in the accusative, thus becoming identical with the dative forms.)

5. Notice the detached prepositions *in* and *ūt* (21). Define the rhetorical force which these prepositions give to the larger syntactical constructions they appear in. To what extent does MnE allow similar constructions? (Cf. German practice, if you can.) Notice also *þurhflēo* (20), *foregange* (26), and *æfterfylige* (27), in which the prepositions are parts of the verbs. Does MnE have forms like these?

6. The essential meanings of *will* and *shall*, and their differences, are made very clear in line 3 (and cf. *woldan*, line 7). Are the distinctions as great in MnE?

7. Find two examples of the plural personal pronoun. Notice that the Scandinavian forms *they, their, them* have not come into the language yet.

8. Notice the comparative degree of the adjectives in lines 28–29. (Later the –*re* > –*er* by metathesis. Other examples are MnE *grass* <OE *gærs* and MnE *bird* <OE *bridd*.)

King Alfred's Prayer

TEXT

Drihten ælmihtiga God, wyrhta ond wealdend
ealra gesceafta, iç bidde þē for þīnre miçelan
mildheortnesse ond for þǣre hālegan rōde tācne,
ond for Sancta Marian mægðhāde, ond for
5 Sancte Michaēles gehȳrsunesse, ond for ealra
þīnra hālgana lufan ond heora earnungum, þæt
þū mē gewissige bet þonne iç āwyrhte tō þē;
ond gewissa mē tō þīnum willan ond tō mīnre
sāwle þearfe bet þonne iç sylf cunne; ond
10 gestaþela mīn mōd tō þīnum willan ond tō
mīnre sāwle þearfe; ond gestranga mē wið þæs
dēofles costnungum; ond āfyrra fram mē þā
fūlan gālnysse ond ælçe unrihtwīsnysse; ond
gescylde mē wið mīnum wiðerwinnum gese-
15 wenlīcum ond ungesewenlīcum; ond tǣç mē
þīnne willan tō wyrçenne, þæt iç mæge þē
inweardlīçe lufian tōforon eallum þingum mid
clǣnum geþance ond mid clǣnum līçhaman;
forþon þe þū eart mīn sceoppend, ond mīn
20 ālēsend, mīn fultum, mīn frōfer, mīn trēwnes,
ond mīn tōhopa; sī þē lof ond wylder nū ond
ā ā ā tō worulde būton æghwilcum ende. Amen.

TRANSCRIPTION

[drɪxtɛn ælmɪxtɪjɑ gɔd wʏrxtɑ ɔnd wæəldɛnd
æəlrɑ jɛšæəftɑ ɪč bɪdɪɛ θeː fɔr θiːnrɛ mɪčɛlɑn
mɪldhɛɔrtnɛsɪɛ ɔnd fɔr θæːrɛ hɑːlɛɣɑn rɔːdɛ
tɑːknɛ ɔnd fɔr sɑŋktɑ mɑrɪɑn mæjθhɑːdɛ ɔnd fɔr
sɑŋktɛ mɪkɑeɪlɛs jɛhyːrzʊnɛsɪɛ ɔnd fɔr æəlrɑ 5
θiːnrɑ hɑːlɣɑnɑ lʊvɑn ɔnd hɛɔrɑ æərnʊŋgʊm
θæt θuː meː jɛwɪsɪɪjɛ bɛt θɔnɪɛ ɪč ɑːwʏrxtɛ toː
θeː ɔnd jɛwɪsɪɑ meː toː θiːnʊm wɪlɪɑn ɔnd toː
miːnrɛ sɑːwlɛ θæərvɛ bɛt θɔnɪɛ ɪč sʏlf kʊnɪɛ
ɔnd jɛstɑðɛlɑ miːn mɔːd toː θiːnʊm wɪlɪɑn ɔnd 10
toː miːnrɛ sɑːwlɛ θæərvɛ ɔnd jɛstrɑŋgɑ meː wɪθ
θæs deːʊvlɛs kɔstnʊŋgʊm ɔnd ɑːfʏrɪɑ frɑm meː
θɑː fuːlɑn gɑːlnysɪɛ ɔnd ælčɛ ʊnrɪxtwiːsnysɪɛ
ɔnd jɛsʏldɛ meː wɪθ miːnʊm wɪðɛrwɪnɪʊm
jɛsɛwɛnliːkʊm ɔnd ʊnjɛsɛwɛnliːkʊm ɔnd tæːč 15
meː θiːnɪɛ wɪlɪɑn toː wʏrčɛnɪɛ θæt ɪč mæjɛ θeː
ɪnwæərdliːčɛ lʊvɪɑn toːfɔrɔn æəlʊm θɪŋgʊm mɪd
klæːnʊm jɛθɑŋkɛ ɔnd mɪd klæːnʊm liːčhɑmɑn
fɔrðɔn θɛ θuː æərt miːn šɛɔpɪɛnd ɔnd miːn
ɑːleːzɛnd miːn fʊltʊm miːn frɔːvɛr miːn treːwnɛs 20
ɔnd miːn toːhɔpɑ siː θeː lɔf ɔnd wʏldɛr nuː ɔnd ɑː
ɑː ɑː toː wɔrʊldɛ buːtɔn æjhwɪlkʊm ɛndɛ ɑmɛn]

TRANSLATION

Lord, Almighty God, master and maker of all creatures, I ask you, by your great mercy and by the holy sign of the cross and by the maidenhood of St. Mary and by the obedience of
5 St. Michael and by the love of all your saints and their merit, (that you) guide me better than I (have) worked for you; and guide me to your will and to the need of my soul better than I can myself; and make my heart stead-
10 fast to your will and to the need of my soul; and strengthen me against the temptations of the devil; and remove from me (the) foul lust and each unrighteousness; and shield me against my adversaries, visible and invisible; and teach
15 me to work your will so that I can love you inwardly before all things with a clean heart and with a clean body; for you are my creator and my redeemer, my help, my solace, my trust, and my hope; love and glory be to you,
20 now and forevermore, world without (any) end. Amen.

EXERCISES

1. This little prayer is a masterpiece of rhetorical prose. What rhetorical devices are used to give it its controlled emotive and artistic force?

2. How many compound nouns can you find in the passage? Which of the nominal suffixes have survived? Find other suffixes in other passages. What do you think are the most active suffixes in MnE?

3. What words have replaced *mildheortnesse* (3), *gehȳrsunesse* (5), and *wiðerwinnum* (14)? From what language(s) have they been borrowed?

4. What prefixes can you find for verbs, adjectives, and nouns in this and preceding selections? Which of these are still active? Which are the most common now?

5. With what modifications in meaning or form have the following words survived into MnE: *miçelan* (2), *mōd* (10), *wið* (11, 14)? (The word *þonne* (7) has become both *than* and *then* in MnE and thus has produced "etymological doublets.")

6. Find an example of the subjunctive mood in the first few lines. What would the form be if it were indicative instead of subjunctive? Why is it subjunctive here?

7. Find several examples of the imperative mood in lines 7–12. (Imperative singular endings are ø, –*e*, or –*a*; imperative plural endings are –(*i*)*an* or –(*i*)*aþ*.)

8. Notice the –*e* ending for the feminine strong noun, genitive singular, exemplified in *rōde* (3) and *sāwle* (9). What ending would you otherwise expect for strong nouns? for weak nouns?

9. What construction is *tō wyrçenne* (16)? What two clues led to your answer? Notice how similar this particular usage is to what we call the "infinitive" in MnE.

p 18
 # 36
(noou)

I insist that he be a good student
is

Attempt to promote the lang. (A reformed orthography)

The Ormulum

ORIGINAL TEXT

þiss boc iss nemmned Orrmulum
  Forrþi þatt Orrm itt wrohhte . . . .

Nu, broþerr Wallterr, broþerr min
  Affterr þe flæshess kinde;
5 Annd broþerr min i Crisstenndom
  þurrh fulluhht annd þurrh trowwþe
Annd broþerr min i Godess hus,
  ʒēt o þe þridde wise,
þurrh þatt witt hafenn tăkenn ba
10 An reʒhellboc to follʒhenn,
Unnderr kanunnkess had annd lif,
  Swa-summ Sannt Awwsten sette;
Icc hafe don swa-summ þu badd
  Annd forþedd te þin wille,
15 Icc hafe wennd inntill Ennglissh
  Goddspelless hallʒhe láre,
Affterr þatt little witt þatt me
  Min Drihhtin hafeþþ lenedd.

    . . .

Annd wha-se wilenn shall þiss boc
20 Efft oþerr siþe writenn,
Himm bidde icc þat hḗ't wríte rihht,
  Swa-summ þiss boc himm tæcheþþ
All þwerrt-ūt affterr þatt itt iss
  Uppo þiss firrste bisne,
25 Wiþþ all swillc ríme alls her iss sett,
  Wiþþ all þe fele wordess;
Annd tatt he loke wel þatt he
  An bocstaff wríte twiʒʒess,
Eʒʒwhær þær itt uppo þiss boc
30 Iss wrítenn o þatt wise.
Loke he wel þatt hḗ't write swa,
  Forr he ne maʒʒ nohht elless
Onn Ennglissh wrítenn rihht te word,
  þatt wite he wel to soþe.

NORMALIZED TEXT

þis bōc is nemmned Ormulum
  Forþi þat Orm it wrohte . . . .

Nū, brōþer Walter, brōþer mīn
  After þe flæshes kīnde;
And brōþer mīn ī Cristendōm   5
  þurh fulluht and þurh trowþe
And brōþer mīn ī Godes hūs,
  ʒēt o þe þridde wīse,
þurh þat wit hāfen taken bā
  An reʒhelbōc tō folʒhen,   10
Under kanunkes hād and līf,
  Swā-sum Sant Awsten sette;
Ic hāfe dōn swā-sum þū bad
  And forþed te þīn wille,
Ic hāfe wend intil Englissh   15
  Godspelles halʒhe lāre,
After þat little wit þat mē
  Mīn Drihtin hāfeþ lēned.

    . . .

And whā-se wilen shall þis bōc
  Eft ōþer siþe wrīten,   20
Him bidde ic þat hē't wrīte riht,
  Swā-sum þis bōc him tæcheþ
All þwert-ūt after þat it is
  Upo þis firste bisne,
Wiþ all swilc rīme als hēr is set,   25
  Wiþ all þe fele wordes;
And tat hē lōke wēl þat hē
  An bōcstaf wrīte twiʒes,
Eʒwhær þær it upo þis bōc
  Is writen o þat wīse.   30
Lōke hē wēl þat hē't wrīte swā,
  For hē ne maʒ noht elles
On Englissh wrīten riht te word,
  þat wite hē wēl tō sōþe.

---

[1] This period lasted from 1100 to 1450. Most of the following works were composed in the late fourteenth century. *The Ormulum*, however, dates from *c.* 1200, and the lyrics from the thirteenth or early fourteenth century.

TRANSCRIPTION

[θɪs boːk ɪs nɛmɪnəd ɔrmʊlʊm
   forðɪ θɑt ɔrm ɪt wrɔxtə

nuː broːðər wɑltər broːðər miːn
   ɑftər θə flæʃəs kiːndə
5 ɑnd broːðər miːn iː krɪstɛndoːm
   θʊrx fʊlːʊxt ɑnd θʊrx trɔʊðə
   ɑnd broːðər miːn iː gɔdəs huːs
   jeːt ɔ θə θrɪdːə wiːzə
   θʊrx θɑt wɪt hɑːvən tɑkən bɑː
10 ɑn rɛɣɛlboːk toː fɔlɣən
   ʊndər kɑnʊŋkəs hɑːd ɑnd liːf
   swɑːsʊm sɑnt ɑʊstən sɛtːə
   ɪč hɑːvə doːn swɑːsʊm θuː bɑd
   ɑnd forðəd tə θiːn wɪlːə
15 ɪč hɑːvə wɛnd ɪntɪl ɛŋglɪš
   gɔdspɛlːəs hɑlɣə lɑːrə
   ɑftər θɑt lɪtːlə wɪt θɑt meː
   miːn drɪxtɪn hɑːvəθ leːnəd

              . . .

   ɑnd hwɑːsə wɪlən šɑl θɪs boːk
20 ɛft oːðər sɪðə wriːtən
   hɪm bɪdːə ɪč θɑt heːt wriːtə rɪxt
   swɑːsʊm θɪs boːk hɪm tæːčəθ
   ɑl θwɛrtuːt ɑftər θɑt ɪt ɪs
   ʊpɔ θɪs fɪrstə bɪznə
25 wɪθ ɑl swɪlč riːm ɑls heːr ɪs sɛt
   wɪθ ɑl θə fɛlə wordəs
   ɑnd tɑt heː loːkə weːl θɑt heː
   ɑn boːkstɑf wriːtə twɪjəs
   æɪhwær θær ɪt ʊpɔ θɪs boːk
30 ɪs wrɪtən ɔ θɑt wiːzə
   loːkə heː weːl θɑt heːt wriːtə swɑː
   for heː nə mæɪ nɔxt ɛlːəs
   ɔn ɛŋglɪš wriːtən rɪxt tə word
   θɑt wɪtə heː weːl toː soːðə]

TRANSLATION

This book is named Ormulum,
   because Orm composed it. . . .

Now, brother Walter, my brother
   after the way of flesh;
and my brother in Christendom   5
   through baptism and through faith,
and my brother in God's house,
   yet in the third way,
because we have both taken
   to follow a monastic rule,   10
according to the rank and life of canon,
   just as St. Augustine established;
I have done as you asked
   and carried (it) out (according) to your will,
I have translated into English   15
   the gospel's holy wisdom,
with the little wit that
   my Lord has granted to me.

              . . .

And whosoever will desire to copy
   this book now and again,   20
I ask (him) that he write it right,
   just as this book shows him
exactly as it is
   in this first model,
with all such rime as is set (down) here,   25
   with all the many words;
and that he look well that he
   write a letter twice
everywhere in this book it
   is written that way.   30
Look well that he write it so,
   for else he cannot
write the word right in English,
   that he knows well, in truth.

EXERCISES

1. Orm (*c.* 1200) was the first English spelling re-
former. In *The Ormulum*, a very long collection of
homilies, he set out to double the consonant after
a short vowel, or, if there are two consonants, to
double the first. He used a single consonant after a
long vowel. Consulting the normalized ME version
opposite Orm's original, as well as the MnE translation, make lists of words to exemplify his attempts
at these three reforms.

2. Make another list showing his own inconsistencies.

3. In general, to what extent does MnE follow Orm's
innovations? Cite specific examples of Orm's innovations which have lasted. Where does MnE not double
consonants where Orm does?

4. Examine a portion of the normalized text very
carefully, word by word, and try to determine for
yourself the extent to which EME has already
simplified orthographically, morphologically, and
syntactically in the two centuries or so after the
composition of the OE texts you have examined.
(The student should regard this early specimen of
the Northeast Midland dialect as transitional, i.e.,
somewhere between OE and ME, and should note
the retention of such OE features as [ɣ], spelled
ȝ—a symbol that also seems to represent [j] in *ȝẽt*,
8, and *twiȝȝess*, 28, and [ɪ] in *eȝȝwhær*, 29, and
maȝȝ, 32—and * æ̆* in *flæshess*, 4, and *tæchepþ*, 22.)

5. How are the unstressed vowels pronounced? How
are the corresponding vowels pronounced in OE?
in MnE?

6. How do the pronunciations of initial and final
th's and *s*'s compare to modern practice?

7. In general, does this passage seem more similar
to OE or to MnE? In what ways: phonologically?
syntactically? morphologically? lexically?

8. How many of the words in the passage have not
survived into MnE?

Geoffrey Chaucer

The General Prologue, 1–72

TEXT

Whan that Āprill with his shoures soǫte
The droghte of March hath pērced tǭ the rǫote,
And bāthed every veyne in swich licour
Of which vertu engendred is the flour;
5   Whan Zephirus ēǫk with his swēǫte brēǫth
Inspīred hath in every holt and hēǫth
The tendre croppes, and the yonge sonne
Hath in the Ram his halve cours yronne,
And smāle foweles māken melodȳe,
10   That slēpen al the nyght with ǭpen ȳe
(Sǭ priketh hem nāture in hir corāges);
Thanne longen folk tǭ gǫon on pilgrimāges,
And palmeres for tǭ sēken straunge strondes,
Tǭ ferne halwes, kowthe in sondry londes;
15   And specially from every shīres ende
Of Engelond tǭ Caunterbury they wende,
The hǫoly blisful martir for tǭ sēke,
That hem hath holpen whan that they wēre
    sēǫke.
    Bifil that in that sēǫson on a day,
20   In Southwerk at the Tabard as Ī lay
Redy tǭ wenden on mȳ pilgrymāge
Tǭ Caunterbury with ful dēvout corāge,
At nyght was come intǭ that hostelrȳe
Wēl nȳne and twenty in a compaignȳe,
25   Of sondry folk, bȳ āventure yfalle
In felaweshipe, and pilgrimes wēre they alle,
That tǭward Caunterbury wǭlden rȳde.
The chāmbres and the stābles wēren wȳde,
And wēl wē wēren ēǫsed atte beste.
30   And shortly, whan the sonne was tǭ reste,
Sǭ hadde Ī spǭken with hem everichǭn
That Ī was of hir felaweshipe anǭn,
And māde forward ērly for tǭ rȳse,
Tǭ tāke oure wey thēr as Ī yow dēvȳse.
35   But nātheleǫs, whīl Ī have tȳme and spāce,
Ēr that Ī ferther in this tāle pāce,
Mē thynketh it acordaunt tǭ rēsoun
Tǭ telle yow al the condicioun
Of ēch of hem, sǭ as it sēmed mē,
40   And whiche they wēren, and of what dēgreǫ,

TRANSCRIPTION

[hwɑn θɑt ɑːprɪl wɪθ ɪs šuːrəs soːtə
θə drʊxt ɔf marč hɑθ peːrsəd toː θə roːtə
ɑnd baːðəd ɛvrɪ væɪn ɪn swɪč lɪkuːr
ɔf hwɪč vɛrtɪʊ ɛnjɛndrəd ɪs θə fluːr
hwɑn zɛfɪrʊs eɪk wɪθ ɪs sweɪtə brɛːθ   5
ɪnspiːrəd hɑθ ɪn ɛvrɪ hɔlt ɑnd hɛːθ
θə tɛndrə krɔpɪəs ɑnd θə jʊŋgə sʊnɪə
hɑθ ɪn θə rɑm ɪs hɑlvə kuːrs ɪrʊnɪə
ɑnd smaːlə fuːləs maːkən mɛlɔdiːə
θɑt sleːpən ɑl θə nɪxt wɪθ ɔːpən iːə   10
sɔː prɪkəθ hɛm naːtiʊr ɪn hɪr kʊraːjəs
θɑn lɔŋgən fɔlk toː gɔɪn ɔn pɪlgrɪmaːjəs
ɑnd palmɛrs fɔr toː seːkən straʊnjə strɔndəs
toː fɛrnə hɑlwəs kuːθ ɪn sʊndrɪ lɔndəs
ɑnd spɛsɪalɪ frɔm ɛvrɪ šiːrəs ɛndə   15
ɔf ɛŋgəlɔnd toː kaʊntərbrɪ θæɪ wɛndə
θə hɔːlɪ blɪsfʊl martɪr fɔr toː seːkə
θɑt hɛm hɑθ hɔlpən hwɑn θɑt θæɪ weːr seːkə
bɪfɪl θɑt ɪn θɑt seɪzuːn ɔn ə dæɪ
ɪn sʊθwɛrk ɑt θə tɑbɑrd ɑs iː læɪ   20
rɛdɪ toː wɛndən ɔn miː pɪlgrɪmaːjə
toː kaʊntərbrɪ wɪθ fʊl deɪvuːt kʊraːjə
ɑt nɪxt wɑs kʊm ɪn toː θɑt ɔstɛlriːə
weɪl niːn ɑnd twɛntɪ ɪn ə kʊmpæɪniːə
ɔf sʊndrɪ fɔlk biː aːvɛntiʊr ɪfɑlɪə   25
ɪn fɛlaʊšɪp ɑnd pɪlgrɪms weːr θæɪ ɑlɪə
θɑt toːwɑrd kaʊntərburɪ wɔːldən riːdə
θə čaːmbrəs ɑnd θə staːbləs weːrən wiːdə
ɑnd weɪl weɪ weːrən ɛːzəd ɑtːə bɛstə
ɑnd šɔrtlɪ hwɑn θə sʊnːə wɑs toː rɛstə   30
sɔː hɑd iː spɔːkən wɪθ ɛm ɛvrɪčɔːn
θɑt iː wɑs ɔf ɪr fɛlaʊšɪp ɑnɔːn
ɑnd maːdə fɔrwɑrd ɛːrlɪ fɔr toː riːzə
toː taːk uːr wæɪ θeːr ɑs iː juː deɪviːzə
bʊt naːðəlɛɪs hwiːl iː hɑv tiːm ɑnd spaːsə   35
ɛːr θɑt iː fɛrðər ɪn θɪs taːlə pɑsə
meɪ θɪŋkəθ ɪt ɑkɔrdaʊnt toː reːzuːn
toː tɛlːə juː ɑl θə kɔndɪsɪuːn
ɔf ɛːč ɔf hɛm sɔː ɑs ɪt seɪməd meɪ
ɑnd hwɪč θæɪ weːrən ɑnd ɔf hwɑt deɪgreː   40
ɑnd eɪk ɪn hwɑt ɑriːæ θɑt θæɪ weːr ɪnɪə

TRANSLATION

When April with its sweet showers
has pierced the drought of March to the root,
and bathed every vein in such liquid
from which strength the flower is engendered;
5 when Zephirus also with his sweet breath
has breathed upon the tender shoots
in every woodland and heath, and the young sun
has run his half-course in the Ram,
and small birds make melody
10 that sleep all the night with open eyes
(so nature pricks them in their hearts);
then folk long to go on pilgrimages,
and palmers, in order to seek foreign shores,
(long to go) to far-off shrines, known in sundry
    lands;
15 and they especially go to Canterbury
from the end of every shire of England
to seek the holy blissful martyr,
who has helped them when they were sick.
    It happened that in that season one day,
20 as I lodged in Southwark at the Tabard,
ready to go on my pilgrimage
to Canterbury with (a) very devout heart,
fully twenty-nine sundry folk
came into that inn in a group,
25 (having) fallen together by chance
into fellowship, and they were all pilgrims
that wanted to ride toward Canterbury.
The rooms and the stables were spacious,
and we were accommodated in the best way.
30 And shortly, when the sun was at rest,
I had spoken with them everyone
so that I was in their fellowship at once,
and (we) made an agreement to rise early
to take our way there as I will describe to you.
35   But nevertheless, while I have time and
        opportunity,
ere I go further in this tale,
it seems to me according to reason
to tell you all (about) the status
of each of them, as it seemed to me,

EXERCISES

1. This selection was written near the end of the fourteenth century. How has ME changed orthographically, morphologically, syntactically, and phonologically since the *Ormulum*?

2. Consult the vowel chart on p. 33, and note carefully the changes that take place in the long vowels from OE to ME times. Find examples in the passage for each of the ME long vowels. Do you notice any changes in the consonants?

3. Compare the OE short vowels to the ME short vowels (see p. 33). Which have changed and which have not? What conclusions can you draw? List examples, drawn from the passage, for each ME short vowel.

4. List the words containing long open $\bar{e}$ [ɛː] and long close $\bar{e}$ [eː]. What rules can you construct to account for the distinction? (Hint: Compare the MnE spelling of these words, if they survive. You may need to cull additional examples from another passage or two of ME in order to have enough evidence.)

5. You might try to do the same thing for ME $\bar{\varrho}$ [ɔː] and $\bar{\varrho}$ [oː], although this is a more difficult problem. (Check your rules with the evidence suggested by the vowel chart, p. 33.)

6. How many of the six ME diphthongs (see. p. 33) can you find in the passage?

7. How many unpronounced final and medial *e*'s can you find here? How do you account for them? (Be specific.) Are final –*e*'s at the ends of lines always pronounced?

8. What optional spelling represents the sound which is also signaled by $\bar{u}$? Does this conform to MnE practice?

9. How different is the word order here from that of MnE poetry? How different is it from that of OE poetry?

10. What part of speech occurs here more often than in *Beowulf* and thereby affects the rhythm of the lines?

11. Scan several lines of the passage and compare

TEXT CONTINUED

And eek in what array that they wēre inne;
And at a knyght than wol Ī first bigynne.
  A KNYGHT thēr was, and that a worthy man,
That frō the tȳme that hē first bigan
45 Tō rīden out, hē loved chivalrīe,
Trouthe and honour, frēdōm and curteisie.
Ful worthy was hē in his lōrdes werre,
And thērtō hadde hē riden, nō man ferre,
As wēl in cristendōm as in hēthenesse,
50 And evere honoured for his worthynesse.
At Alisaundre hē was whan it was wonne.
Ful ofte tȳme hē hadde the bōrd bigonne
Aboven alle nācions in Pruce;
In Lettow hadde hē reysed and in Ruce,
55 Nō Cristen man sō ofte of his dēgrēe.
In Gernāde at the sēege eek hadde hē bē
Of Algezir, and riden in Belmarye.
At Lȳeys was hē and at Satalȳe,
Whan they wēre wonne; and in the Grēte Sēe
60 At many a nōble armēe hadde hē bē.
At mortal batailles hadde hē bēen fiftēne,
And foughten for oure feith at Tramyssēne
In lystes thrīes, and ay slayn his foo.
This ilke worthy knyght hadde bēen alsō
65 Somtȳme with the lōrd of Palatȳe
Agayn anōther hēthen in Turkȳe.
And everemōore hē hadde a sovereyn prȳs;
And though that hē wēre worthy, hē was wȳs,
And of his port as mēeke as is a mayde.
70 Hē nevere yet nō vileynȳe ne sayde
In al his lȳf untō nō maner wight.
Hē was a verray, parfit gentil knyght.

TRANSCRIPTION CONTINUED

ɑnd ɑt ə knɪxt θɑn wɔl iː fɪrst bɪgɪnɪə
  ə knɪxt θɛɪr wɑs ɑnd θɑt ə wǒrðɪ mɑn
θɑt frɔː θə tiːmə θɑt eɪ fɪrst bɪgɑn
toː riːdən uɪt eɪ lʊvəd čɪvɑlriːə   45
trɔʊθ ɑnd ɔnuɪr freɪdoːm ɑnd kʊrtæɪziːə
fʊl wǒrðɪ wɑs eɪ ɪn ɪs lɔɪrdəs werːə
ɑnd θɛɪrtoː hɑd eɪ rɪdən nɔː mɑn ferːə
ɑs weɪl ɪn krɪstəndoːm ɑs ɪn hɛɪðənɛsːə
ɑnd ɛvr ɔnuɪrəd fɔr ɪs wǒrðɪnɛsːə   50
ɑt ɑlɪsɑʊndr eɪ wɑs hwɑn ɪt wɑs wʊnːə
fʊl ɔftə tiːm eɪ hɑd θə bɔɪrd bɪgʊnːə
ɑbʊvən ɑlːə nɑːsɪuɪns ɪn prɪʊsə
ɪn lɛtɔʊ hɑd eɪ ræɪzəd ɑnd ɪn rɪʊsə
nɔː krɪstən mɑn sɔː ɔft ɔf hɪs deɪgreɪ   55
ɪn gɛrnɑːd ɑt θə seɪǰ eɪk hɑd eɪ beɪ
ɔf ɑlǰezɪr ɑnd rɪdən ɪn belmɑriːə
ɑt liːæɪs wɑs eɪ ɑnd ɑt sɑtɑliːə
hwɑn θæɪ weɪr wʊn ɑnd ɪn θə grɛɪtə seɪ
ɑt mɑnɪ ə nɔɪbəl ɑrmeɪ hɑd eɪ beɪ   60
ɑt mɔrtɑl bɑtæɪls hɑd eɪ beɪn fɪfteɪnə
ɑnd fɔʊxtən fɔr uɪr fæɪθ ɑt trɑmɪseɪnə
ɪn lɪstəs θriːəs ɑnd æɪ slæɪn ɪs fɔɪ
θɪs ɪlkə wǒrðɪ knɪxt hɑd beɪn ɑlsɔː
sʊmtiːmə wɪθ θə lɔɪrd ɔf pɑlɑtiːə   65
ɑgæɪn ɑnɔɪðər hɛɪðən ɪn tʊrkiːə
ɑnd ɛvərmɔɪr eɪ hɑd ə sʊvræɪn priːs
ɑnd θɔʊx θɑt heɪ weɪr wǒrðɪ heɪ wɑs wiːs
ɑnd ɔf ɪs pɔrt ɑs meɪk ɑs ɪs ə mæɪdə
heɪ nɛvrə jet nɔɪ vɪlæɪniː nə sæɪdə   70
ɪn ɑl ɪs liːf ʊntɔɪ nɔɪ mɑnər wɪxt
heɪ wɑs ə verːæɪ pɑrfɪt ǰentɪl knɪxt]

TRANSLATION CONTINUED

40 and who they were, and of what rank,
and also in what dress they were in;
and with a knight, then, I will first begin.
   There was a knight, and that (was) a worthy
       man,
who from the time that he first began
45 to ride forth he loved chivalry,
   fidelity and honor, generosity and courtly be-
       havior.
He was very worthy in his lord's war,
and no man had ridden farther thereto (than) he,
in Christendom as well as in heathen countries,
50 and (he was) ever honored for his worthiness.
He was at Alexandria when it was won.
He had very often sat at the head of the table
above all nations in Prussia;
no Christian man of his rank had campaigned
55 as often as he in Lithuania and in Russia;
he had also been in Granada at the siege
of Algeciras and (had) ridden in Benmarin.
He was at Ayas and at Attalia
when they were won; and he had been
60 on the Great Sea with many a noble army.
He had been in fifteen mortal battles,
and (had) fought for our faith in three lists
at Tremessen, and (had) always slain his foe.
This same worthy knight had also been
65 for a time with the lord of Palathia
against another heathen in Turkey.
And, ever since, he had the highest reputation;
and though he was worthy, he was wise,
and in his bearing (he was) as meek as a maid.
70 He (has) never yet said anything villainous
in all his life to any sort of person.
He was a true, perfect, courteous knight.

EXERCISES CONTINUED

the rhythm with that in *Beowulf*. What differences
do you note? How are they to be accounted for?

12. How much difference is there between the
rhythm of these lines and the corresponding lines
of the MnE translation? What conclusion(s) about
the development of the language can you draw?

13. Does the prosody you find here suggest that
ME poetry is more like that of modern poetry or of
OE poetry? Explain.

14. What form of the third person singular pronoun

does Chaucer consistently use for the neuter possessive *its*? Note that this is the same form used in
OE and that its use continues into the EMnE
period, when the alternate forms *it* and then *it's*
(with the apostrophe) also come into use. It isn't
until the eighteenth century that the modern form
its comes into use.

15. Note carefully the pronunciation of such French
borrowings as *engendred* (4), *tendre* (7), and *pilgrimāges* (12). The beginning student often makes
the words sound like modern French, thus attribut-
ing sounds to OF that have not yet developed.

16. Make a list of all the French borrowings in this
passage (and perhaps in the two following this one)
and, by paying close attention to the general pattern
of iambic pentameter in Chaucer's lines, indicate
where primary stress occurs. In how many of these
words has the primary stress shifted since Chaucer
wrote? When the shift occurs, is it always in the
same direction? Why?

17. To what extent and in what ways has the language been affected by French accentuation due to
the heavy influx of the French borrowings which
followed the Norman Conquest and reached a peak
in Chaucer's time? You will doubtless want to
reexamine OE metrics to answer this question.

18. Comment on each of the following usages, and
explain how each differs from present-day usage:

> *Whan that* (1, 18)
> *from every shīres ende/Of Engelond* (15–16)
> *for tō sēke(n)* (13, 17)
> *mē thinketh* (37)
> *it sēmed mē* (39)
> *at* (60, 61)
> *lystes thrīes* (63)
> *nevere . . . nǭ . . . ne . . . /nǭ* (70–71)

19. Note carefully the following ME words, and
explain the extent to which each has subsequently
changed in form, pronunciation, and meaning:

licour (3)	*whiche* (40)
inspīred (6)	*knyght* (42)
foweles (9)	*trouthe* (cf. *troth*) (46)
corāges (11)	*honour* (46)
halwes (14)	*frēdōm* (46)
anōn (32)	*curteisīe* (46)
ferther (36)	*dēgrēē* (55)
ferre (48)	*ilke* (64)
	verray (72)

Geoffrey Chaucer

Troilus and Criseyde I, 1–28

TEXT

The double sorwe of Troilus tọ tellen,
That was the kyng Prīamus sone of Troye,
In lovynge, how his āventures fellen
Frọ wọ tọ wẹle, and after out of joie,
5 Mȳ purpos is, ẹr that Ī parte frọ yẹ.
Thesiphone, thow help mẹ for t'endīte
Thise wọful vers, that wẹpen as Ī wrīte.

Tọ thẹ clẹpe Ī, thow goddesse of torment,
Thow cruwel Furie, sorwynge ẹvere yn peyne,
10 Help mẹ, that am the sorwful instrument,
That helpeth loveres, as Ī kan, tọ pleyne.
For wẹl sit it, the sọthe for tọ seyne,
A wọful wight tọ han a drẹry fẹere,
And tọ a sorwful tāle, a sọry chẹre.

15 For Ī, that God of Loves servantz serve,
Ne dār tọ Love, for mȳn unlīklynesse,
Preyen for spẹẹd, al shọlde Ī thẹrfore sterve,
Sọ fer am Ī from his help in derknesse.
But nāthelẹs, if this may dọn gladnesse
20 Tọ any lovere, and his cause availle,
Have hẹ mȳ thonk, and mȳn bẹ this travaille!

But yẹ loveres, that bāthen in gladnesse,
If any drope of pytẹ in yow bẹ,
Remembreth yow on passed hevynesse
25 That yẹ han felt, and on the adversitẹ
Of ọthere folk, and thynketh how that yẹ
Han felt that Love dorste yow displẹse,
Or yẹ han wonne hym with tọ grẹt an ẹse.

TRANSCRIPTION

[θə duːblə sɔrwəf trɔɪlʊs toː tɛlɪən
θat was θə kɪŋg priːamʊs sʊn ɔf trɔɪə
ɪn lʊvɪŋg huː ɪs aːvɛntiʊrəs fɛlɪən
froː wɔː toː wɛːl and aftər uːt ɔf jɔɪə
miː pʊrpɔs ɪs ɛːr θat iː part frɔː jeː   5
tɛsɪfɔnə θuː hɛlp meː fɔr tɛndiːtə
θɪs wɔːfʊl vɛrs θat wɛːpən as iː wriːtə

toː θeː klɛːp iː θuː gɔdɪɛs ɔf tɔrmɛnt
θuː krɪʊəl fiʊriː sɔrwɪŋg ɛːvrɪn pæɪnə
hɛlp meː θat am θə sɔrwfʊl ɪnstrʊmɛnt   10
θat hɛlpəθ lʊvərs as iː kan toː plæɪnə
fɔr wɛːl sɪt ɪt θə soːðə fɔr toː sæɪnə
ə wɔːfʊl wɪxt toː han ə dreːrɪ fɛːrə
and toː ə sɔrwfʊl taɪl ə sɔːrɪ čɛːrə

fɔr iː θat gɔd ɔf lʊvəs sɛrvants sɛrvə   15
nə daːr toː lʊv fɔr miːn ʊnliːklɪnɛsɪə
præɪən fɔr speːd al šoːld iː θɛːrfɔr stɛrvə
sɔː fɛr am iː frɔm hɪs hɛlp ɪn dɛrknɛsɪə
bʊt naːðəlɛːs ɪf θɪs mæɪ doɪn gladnɛsɪə
toː anɪ lʊvər and ɪs kaʊs aʋæɪlɪə   20
haʋ heː miː θɔŋk and miːn beː θɪs traʋæɪlɪə

bʊt jeː lʊvərs θat baːðən ɪn gladnɛsɪə
ɪf anɪ drɔp ɔf piːteː ɪn juː beː
rɛmɛmbrəθ juː ɔn pasɪəd hɛvɪnɛsɪə
θat jeː han fɛlt and ɔn θadvɛrsɪteː   25
ɔf oːðər fɔlk and θɪŋkəθ huː θat jeː
han fɛlt θat lʊv dʊrst juː dɪsplɛːzə
ɔr jeː han wɔn ɪm wɪθ toː grɛːt an ɛːzə]

TRANSLATION

My purpose is, ere I depart from you,
to tell the double sorrow
in loving of Troilus, who was the son of
King Priamus of Troy—how his fortunes fell
5 from woe to happiness, and afterwards (fell)
out of joy.
Tisiphone, (thou) help me to compose
these woeful verses that weep as I write.

I call to thee, thou goddess of torment,
thou cruel Fury, ever sorrowing in pain,
10 help me, who am the sorrowful instrument,
who helps lovers, as I can, to lament.
For it is very fitting, to tell the truth,
(for) a woeful fellow to have a sad companion,
and a mournful face (is very fitting) to a sorrowful tale.

15 For I, who serve the God of Love's servants,
dare not, on account of my hopelessness,
pray to Love for success, although I might die
for it,
so far am I from his help in darkness.
But nevertheless, if this can cause happiness
20 for any lover, and help his cause,
(may) he have my thanks, and (may) this travail
be mine.

But you lovers, who bathe in happiness,
if any drop of pity is in you,
remember past sorrow
25 that you have felt, and the adversity
of other folk, and think how you
have felt (when you recall) that love dared dis-
please you,
or (else) you (would) have won him with too
great ease.

EXERCISES

1. Using a dictionary, determine how many of the nouns and adjectives in the first two stanzas are borrowed from other languages. From which language particularly? By comparison, what percentage of foreign words does OE have?

2. In this and other ME passages, find examples of *gh* spellings in words. Look up the etymology of the words and determine how the *gh*'s were spelled in OE. What is the MnE spelling? Carry out the same investigation for the following ME spellings, remembering that some ME letters are derived from more than one source: *c(c)h*, *s(s)h*, *g*, *gg*, *y* (the consonant), *qu–*, *hw–*. (Also, look up the etymology of *ring*, *link*, and *neck* and make notes on the history of the spelling of each.)

3. Is a spelling distinction made between short vowels and long vowels in ME? (The diacritical marks are editorial.) Is the distinction made in OE? in MnE? What about the subsequent development of these vowels helps you determine their length in ME?

4. Are ME long vowels consistently doubled?

5. Referring to the vowel triangles on p. 22, note the ME long vowels that do not occur in OE and find examples in the passage above. Which of the new vowel sounds are developments from other OE vowels? Which OE long vowels do not appear in ME? Are there more or fewer long vowels in ME than in OE?

6. Which OE short vowels do not occur in ME? Do any new short vowels occur in ME? Why? Are there more or fewer short vowels in ME than in OE? Find examples of each ME short vowel in the passage above. How many of these vowels appear in MnE unchanged? Can you tell from the selection above (and from its phonetic transcription) which two short vowels in ME have variant spellings? Which two long vowels have variant spellings (beside the usual option of doubling the vowels)? Consult additional selections whenever this one doesn't afford sufficient evidence.

7. What four sounds in ME does the letter *o* represent? What three sounds does the letter *e* represent? Find an example of each.

8. Find examples of the ME diphthong which does not develop from an OE sound but is acquired by borrowing foreign words with the sound in it (see vowel chart, p. 33).

Geoffrey Chaucer

Troilus and Criseyde V, 1786–1841

TEXT

   Gǭ, lītel bǭk, gǭ, lītel mȳn tragedȳe,
   Thę̄r God thī mākere yet, er that hę̄ dȳe,
   Sǭ sende myght tǭ māke in som comedȳe!
   But lītel bǭk nǭ mākyng thow n'envīe,
5   But subgit bę̄ tǭ alle pǭesȳe;
   And kis the steppes, whę̄re as thow sę̄st pāce
   Virgile, Ō̧vide, Ō̧mer, Lūcan, and Stāce.

   And for thę̄r is sǭ grę̄t diversitę̄
   In Englissh and in wrītyng of oure tonge,
10 Sǭ prey Ī God that non myswrīte thę̄,
   Ne thę̄ mysmę̄tre for dę̄faute of tonge.
   And rę̄d whę̄rsǭ thow bę̄, or elles songe,
   That thow bę̄ understonde, God Ī bisę̄che!
   But yet tǭ purpos of mȳ rāther spę̄che.—

change in meaning

15 The wrāth, as Ī bigan yow for tǭ seye,
   Of Troilus the Grę̄kis boughten dę̄ere.
   For thousandes his hondes māden deye,
   As hę̄ that was withouten any pę̄ere,
   Sāve Ector, in his tȳme, as Ī kan hę̄ere.
20 But weilawey, sāve only Goddes wille!
   Despitously hym slough the fierse Achille.

   And whan that hę̄ was slayn in this manę̄re,
   His lighte gǭost ful blisfully is went
   Up tǭ the holughnesse of the eighthe spę̄re,
25 In convers letyng everich element;
   And thę̄r hę̄ saugh, with ful avȳsement,
   The erratik sterres, herkenyng armonȳe
   With sownes ful of hevenyssh melodīe.

   And down from thennes faste hę̄ gan avȳse
30 This lītel spot of ę̄rthe, that with the sę̄
   Embrāced is, and fully gan despīse
   This wrecched world, and held al vaṅitę̄
   Tǭ respect of the pleyn felicitę̄
   That is in hevene above; and at the laste,
35 Thę̄r hę̄ was slayn, his lokyng down hę̄ caste.

   And in hymself hę̄ lough right at the wǭ

TRANSCRIPTION

[gɔː liːtəl boːk gɔː liːtəl miːn traǰədiːə
θeːr gɔd θiː maːkər jɛt ɛr θɑt eː diːə
sɔː sɛndə mɪxt toː maːk ɪn sɔm kɔmədiːə
but liːtəl boːk nɔː maːkɪŋ θuː nɛnviːə
but subjɪt beː toː ɑlːə pɔːesiːə   5
ɑnd kɪs θə stɛpːəs hwɛːr ɑs θuː seːst pɑːsə
vɪrjɪl ɔːvɪd ɔːmɛr luːkɑn ɑnd stɑːsə

ɑnd fɔr θeːr ɪs sɔː greːt dɪvɛrsɪteː
ɪn ɛŋglɪš ɑnd ɪn wriːtɪŋ ɔf uːr tɔŋgə
sɔː præi iː gɔd θɑt nɔn mɪswriːtə θeː   10
nɛ θeː mɪsmeːtrə fɔr deːfɑut ɔf tɔŋgə
ɑnd reːd hwɛːrsɔː θuː beː ɔr ɛlːəs sɔŋgə
θɑt θuː beː ʊndɛrstɔndə gɔd iː bɪseːčə
but jɛt toː purpɔs ɔf miː raːðər speːčə

θə wraːθ ɑs iː bɪgɑn juː fɔr toː sæiə   15
ɔf trɔɪlʊs θə greːkɪs bɔuxtən dɛːrə
fɔr θuːzɑndəs ɪs hɔndəs maːdən dæiə
ɑs heː θɑt wɑs wɪðuːtən ɑnɪ peːrə
sɑːv ɛktɔr ɪn ɪs tiːm ɑs iː kɑn heːrə
but wæilɑwæi sɑːv ɔnlɪ gɔdːəs wɪlːə   20
dɛspɪtuːslɪ ɪm slɑu θə fɛrs ɑkɪlːə

ɑnd hwɑn θɑt heː wɑs slæin ɪn θɪs mɑneːrə
hɪs lɪxtə gɔːst fʊl blɪsfʊlɪ ɪs wɛnt
ʊp toː θə hɔlʊxnəs ɔf θə æixθə speːrə
ɪn kɔnvɛrs lɛtɪŋ ɛvrɪč ɛləmɛnt   25
ɑnd θeːr eː sɑux wɪθ fʊl aviːzəmɛnt
θɛrːɑtɪk stɛrːəs hɛrknɪŋ ɑrmɔniːə
wɪθ suːnəs fʊl ɔf hɛvnɪš mɛlɔdiːə

ɑnd duːn frɔm θɛnːəs fɑst eː gɑn aviːzə
θɪs liːtəl spɔt ɔf eːrθ θɑt wɪθ θə sɛː   30
ɛmbraːsəd ɪs ɑnd fʊlːɪ gɑn dɛspiːzə
θɪs wrɛčəd wɔrld ɑnd hɛld ɑl vɑnɪteː
toː rɛspɛkt ɔf θə plæin fɛlɪsɪteː
θɑt ɪs ɪn hɛvn ɑbʊv ɑnd ɑt θə lɑstə
θeːr heː wɑs slæin ɪs lɔkɪŋ duːn eː kɑstə   35

ɑnd ɪn hɪmself heː lɔux rɪxt ɑt θə wɔː

TRANSLATION

Go little book; go my little tragedy,
so that before he die, God, thy maker still,
may send (him) strength to match (you with)
    some comedy.
But, little book, do not be envious of other
    poetry,
5 but be a subject for all poetry,
and kiss the steps where you see
Virgil, Ovid, Homer, Lucan, and Statius pass.

And since there is such great diversity
in English and in the writing of our speech,
10 I pray God that none miswrite you,
or mismeter you because of lack of ability.
And wherever you are read, or else sung,
I beseech God that you be understood.
But again to the purpose of my earlier speech:

15 As I began to tell you, the Greeks
paid dearly for the wrath of Troilus.
For his hands made thousands die,
since he was without peer,
except for Hector, in his time, as (far as) I can
    hear.
20 But alas, only because of God's will,
the fierce Achilles spitefully slew him.

And after he has been slain in this manner,
his light spirit has gone very blissfully
up to the concavity of the eighth sphere,
25 leaving behind every element;
and there he saw, with much contemplation,
the erratic stars, hearing harmony
with sounds full of heavenly melody.

And down from thence he rapidly began to
    consider
30 this little spot of earth that is embraced
by the sea, and began fully to despise
this wretched world, and considered everything
    vanity

EXERCISES

1. In late OE, short vowels usually lengthen before
–ld, –nd, and –mb (see p. 21). Find examples of long
vowels before these consonant clusters in this and
other ME selections, noting as well exceptions to
the rule.

2. EME long vowels are shortened before two consonants or before a double consonant, in the first
syllable of trisyllabic words, and in unstressed
syllables (see p. 21). Can you find manifestations
of these shortenings in this and other ME selections?

3. In the thirteenth century, the short vowels a, e, o
were lengthened in open syllables of disyllabic words.
(See p. 22; an open syllable is a syllable which ends
in a vowel.) Can you find examples in the ME
selections? (In order to be sure that the vowels were
short in OE, you would have to consult an OE
glossary.)

4. Comparing ME passages with their translations,
what inconsistencies in spelling can you find? What
letter is particularly troublesome?

5. Notice the first example of the subjunctive in
this passage. Are we likely to use this particular
construction very much in MnE? Find other syntactic constructions, here and in the other selections,
that would seem archaic (or dialectical) today.

6. Examine this and the other ME passages for
noun inflections. What forms do you find? In what
specific ways do the endings differ from OE and
from MnE? (List the OE forms of the nominative,
genitive, dative, and accusative, and the ME and
MnE forms alongside.)

7. How does the ME writer express the possessive
singular? How can we express it in MnE?

8. In OE, nouns of relationship such as brother and
father (i.e., brōðor and fæder) have no ending for
the genitive singular. Find a similar example in
ME in the Prodigal Son passage below. By ME
times, other nouns sometimes, though not regularly,
reflect the same lack of possessive inflection. Find
an example in the first Troilus and Criseyde passage.
(Is there another possible reason for the lack of

TEXT CONTINUED

Of hem that wepten for his dēth sǭ faste;
And dampned al oure werk that foloweth sǭ
The blȳnde lust, the which that may nat laste,
40 And sholden al oure herte on heven caste.
And forth hē wente, shortly for tǫ telle,
Thēr as Mercurye sorted hym tǫ dwelle.

Swich fȳn hath, lǭ, this Troilus for love!
Swich fȳn hath al his grēte worthynesse!
45 Swich fȳn hath his estāt real above,
Swich fȳn his lust, swich fȳn hath his nǭblesse!
Swych fȳn hath false worldes brotelnesse!
And thus bigan his lovyng of Criseyde,
As Ī have told, and in this wīse hē deyde.

50 Ǭ yonge, fresshe folkes, hē or shē,
In which that love up grǭweth with youre āge,
Repeyreth hǫm frǭ worldly vanytē,
And of youre herte up casteth the visāge
Tǭ thilke God that after his ymāge
55 Yow māde, and thynketh al nys but a faire
This world, that passeth sǫǫne as floures faire.

TRANSCRIPTION CONTINUED

ɔf hɛm θɑt wɛptən fɔr ɪs dɛːθ sɔː fɑstə
ɑnd dɑmpned ɑl uːr wɛrk θɑt fɔlwəθ sɔː
θə bliːndə lʊst θə hwɪč θɑt mæːɪ nɑt lɑstə
ɑnd šɔldən ɑl uːr hɛrt ɔn hɛvən kɑstə   40
ɑnd fɔrθ eː wɛntə šɔrtlɨ fɔr tɔː tɛlːə
θɛːr ɑs mɛrkrɨ sɔrted hɪm tɔː dwɛlːə

swɪč fiːn hɑθ lɔː θɪs trɔɪlʊs fɔr lʊvə
swɪč fiːn hɑθ ɑl ɪs grɛːtə wʊrðɨnɛsːə
swɪč fiːn hɑθ hɪs estaːt rɛɑl ɑbʊvə   45
swɪč fiːn ɪs lʊst swɪč fiːn hɑθ hɪs nɔːblɛsːə
swɪč fiːn hɑθ fɑlsə wɔrldəs brɔtəlnɛsːə
ɑnd θʊs bɪgɑn ɪs lʊvɪŋg ɔf krɪsæːɪdə
ɑs iː hɑv tɔld ɑnd ɪn θɪs wiːz eː dæːɪdə

ɔː jʊngə frɛšə fɔlkəs heː ɔr šeː   50
ɪn hwɪč θɑt lʊv ʊp grɔːwəθ wɪθ juːr ɑːɪjə
rɛpæːɪrəθ hɔːm frɔː wɔrldlɨ vɑnɨteː
ɑnd ɔf juːr hɛrt ʊp kɑstəθ θə vɪsɑːɪjə
tɔː θɪlkə gɔd θɑt ɑftɛr hɪs ɪmɑːɪjə
juː mɑːd ɑnd θɪŋkəθ ɑl nɪs bʊt ə fæːɪrə   55
θɪs wɔrld θɑt pɑsːəθ sɔːn ɑs fluːɪrəs fæːɪrə]

TRANSLATION CONTINUED

in comparison to the perfect felicity
that is in heaven above; and at last
35   he cast his gaze down where he was slain.

And he laughed to himself at the woe
of them that wept for his death so quick,
and condemned all our activity that results from
blind lust, which cannot last,
40   and (when we) should direct all our hearts to
      heaven.
And he went forth—to speak quickly—
where Mercury directed him to dwell.

Lo, such an end Troilus has for love.
Such an end all his greatness has.
45   Such an end his high royal rank has.
Such an end his lust, such an end his nobility has.
Such an end the false world's fragility has.
And thus his loving of Criseyde began,
as I have narrated, and in this way he died.

50   O young, lively folk, (whether) he or she,
in whom love grows with age,
return home from worldly vanity,
and turn your heart
to the same God who made you
55   in his image, and consider that this world is
      nothing
but a fair that passes as quickly as fair flowers.

EXERCISES CONTINUED

inflection in this instance?) Does this sort of construction survive into MnE? (Look up the etymology of *ladybird* and *ladybug*.)

9. Some OE words which have no ending for the plural survive into Chaucer. Find an example in the selection before this one and another in *A Treatise on the Astrolabe* below. How many MnE nouns can you think of with no inflection for the plural? Think especially of constructions similar to the one in *A Treatise on the Astrolabe*.

10. Find a nominal suffix that recurs in the selection and that is also active in OE as well as MnE. Find an adjectival ending that is not active in MnE.

11. In what form does the OE infinitive survive in ME? How has the OE preterit plural ending been modified? What general principle of sound change do these specific modifications demonstrate?

12. What precisely has happened to the OE present participial ending?

13. Study the other verb forms in this and the preceding selection and compare them with the way they would appear in OE. (Cf. pp. 41–43, especially #14.) Can you account for the changes? Note particularly the third person singular and plural forms.

Geoffrey Chaucer

A Treatise on the Astrolabe, 1–49

TEXT

Lȳte Lowys mȳ sone, Ī aperceyve wẹl bȳ certeyne evydences thȳn abilitẹ tọ lẹrne scīences
touching nombres and proporciouns; and as wẹl
considre Ī thȳ besy praier in special tọ lẹrne the
5 trẹtys of the Astrelabīe. Than for as mochel as a
philosofre saith, "hẹ wrappith him in his frẹnd,
that condescendith tọ the rightfulle praiers of his
frẹnd," thẹrfore have Ī yeven thẹ a suffisant
Astrolabīe as for oure orizonte, compowned after
10 the latitude of Oxenfọrde; upon which, bȳ
mediācioun of this lītel trẹtys, Ī purpose tọ
tẹche thẹ a certein nombre of conclūsions aper-
teynyng tọ the sāme instrument. Ī seie a certein
of conclūsions, for thrẹ causes. The first cause is
15 this: truste wẹl that alle the conclūsions that han
bẹ founde, or ellys possibly might bẹ founde in
sọ nọble an instrument as is an Astrelabīe bẹn
unknọwe parfitly tọ eny mortal man in this rẹ-
gioun, as Ī suppọse. Anọther cause is this, that
20 sọthly in any trẹtis of the Astrelabīe that Ī have
seyn, thẹre bẹ somme conclūsions that wol not
in alle thinges parformen her bihestes; and
somme of hem bẹn tọ harde tọ thȳ tendir āge
of ten yẹẹr tọ conceyve.

25 This trẹtis, divīded in 5 partīes, wol Ī shewe
thẹ under full light reules and nāked wordes in
Englissh, for Latȳn ne canst thou yit but small,
mȳ lītel sone. But nāthelẹs suffise tọ thẹ thẹse
trewe conclūsions in Englissh as wẹl as sufficith
30 tọ thẹse nọble clerkes Grẹkes thẹse sāme conclūsions in Grẹk; and tọ Arābiens in Arabik,
and tọ Jewes in Ẹbrew, and tọ the Latȳn folk
in Latȳn; whiche Latȳn folk had hem first out
of ọthere dȳverse langāges, and writen hem in
35 her owne tunge, that is tọ seyn, in Latȳn. And
God wọot that in alle thẹse langāges and in
many mọọ han thẹse conclūsions bẹn suffisantly
lẹrned and taught, and yit bȳ dīversè reules;
right as dīverse pāthes lẹden dīverse folk the
40 righte way tọ Rọme. Now wol Ī preie mẹkely
ẹvery discrẹt persone that rẹdith or hẹrith this
lītel trẹtys tọ have mȳ rude endītyng for ex-

TRANSCRIPTION

[liːtə luːɪs miː sʊn iː ɑpersiːv weːl biː sɛrtæɪn
ɛvidɛnsəs θiːn ɑbɪlɪteː toː leɪrn siːɛnsəs tuːčɪŋ
nʊmbrəs ɑnd prɔpɔrsiuːns ɑnd ɑs weɪl kɔnsɪdrə
iː θiː bɛzɪ præɪr ɪn spɛsiɑl toː leɪrn θə trɛːtɪs
5 ɔf θə ɑstrɛlɑbiːə θɑn fɔr ɑs mʊčəl ɑs ə fɪlɔsɔfrə
sæɪθ heː wrɑpɪːθ hɪm ɪn ɪs freɪnd θɑt kɔndɛ-
sɛndɪθ toː θə rɪxtfʊl præɪrs ɔf ɪs freɪnd θɛɪrfɔr
hɑv iː jɛvən θeɪ ə sufɪːsɑnt ɑstrɔlɑbiːə ɑs fɔr uːr
ɔrɪzɔnt kɔmpuːnəd ɑftər θə lɑtɪtiʊd ɔf ɔksɛnfɔɪrd
10 ʊpɔn hwɪč biː mediɑɪsiuːn ɔf θɪs liːtəl trɛːtɪs iː
pʊrpɔs toː tɛɪč θeɪ ə sɛrtæɪn nʊmbrə ɔf kɔnklu-
ziuːns ɑpertæɪnɪŋ toː θə sæɪm ɪnstrʊmɛnt iː
sæɪ ə sɛrtæɪn ɔf kɔnkluːziuːns fɔr θrɛɪ kɑʊzəs
θə fɪrst kɑʊz ɪs θɪs trʊst weɪl θɑt ɑl θə kɔnkluː-
15 ziuːns θɑt hɑn beɪ fuːnd ɔr ɛliːs pɔsɪːblɪ mɪxt
beɪ fuːnd ɪn sɔɪ nɔɪbl ɑn ɪnstrʊmɛnt ɑs ɪs ɑn
ɑstrɛlɑbiːə beɪn ʊnknɔʊn pɑrfɪtlɪ toː ɛnɪ mɔrtɑl
mɑn ɪn θɪs reɪjiuːn ɑs iː sʊpɔɪz ɑnoɪðər kɑʊz
ɪs θɪs θɑt sɔɪðlɪ ɪn ɑnɪ trɛɪtɪs ɔf θə ɑstrɛlɑbiːə
20 θɑt iː hɑv sæɪn θeɪr beɪ sʊm kɔnkluːziuːns θɑt
wɔl nɔt ɪn ɑl θɪŋgəs pɑrfɔrmən hɛr bɪhɛstəs
ɑnd sʊm ɔf hɛm beɪn toɪ hɑrd toɪ θiː tɛndɪr ɑɪj
ɔf tɛn jeɪr toɪ kɔnsiːv

θɪs trɛːtɪs dɪviːdəd ɪn fiːv pɑrtiːəs wɔl iː šɛʊ
25 θeɪ ʊndər fʊl lɪxt rɛʊləs ɑnd nɑɪkəd wɔrdəs ɪn
ɛŋglɪš fɔr lɑtiːn nə kɑnst θuɪ jɪt bʊt smɑl miː
liːtəl sʊn bʊt nɑɪðeleɪs sufiːs toɪ θeɪ θeɪz triʊ
kɔnkluːziuːns ɪn ɛŋglɪš ɑs weɪl ɑs sufiːsiθ toɪ
θeɪz nɔɪblə klɛrkəs greɪkəs θeɪz sæɪm kɔnkluː-
30 ziuːns ɪn greɪk ɑnd toɪ ɑrɑɪbiɛns ɪn ɑrɑbik ɑnd
toɪ jiʊs ɪn eɪbrɛʊ ɑnd toɪ θə lɑtiːn fɔlk ɪn lɑtiːn
hwɪč lɑtiːn fɔlk hɑd hɛm fɪrst uɪt ɔf oɪðər
diːvers lɑŋgɑɪjəs ɑnd wrɪtən hɛm ɪn hɛr ɔʊn tʊŋg
θɑt ɪs toɪ sæɪn ɪn lɑtiːn ɑnd gɔd wɔɪt θɑt ɪn ɑl
35 θɛɪz lɑŋgɑɪjəs ɑnd ɪn mɑnɪ mɔɪ hɑn θɛɪz kɔnkluː-
ziuːns beɪn sufɪːsɑntlɪ leɪrnəd ɑnd tɑʊxt ɑnd
jɪt biɪ diːvers rɛʊləs rɪxt ɑs diːvers pɑɪðəs leɪdən
diːvers fɔlk θə rɪxt wæɪ toɪ rɔɪm nuɪ wɔl iː præɪ
meɪkəlɪ ɛɪvərɪ dɪskreɪt pɛrsɔn θɑt rɛɪdɪθ ɔr
40 hɛɪrɪθ θɪs liːtəl trɛːtɪs toɪ hɑv miː riʊd endɪːtɪŋg
fɔr ɛkskiʊsɪd ɑnd miː suɪpɛrfluːɪteɪ ɔf wɔrdəs
fɔr twɔɪ kɑʊzes θə fɪrst kɑʊz ɪs fɔr θɑt kiʊriuːs

[handwritten notes in top margin: #5) 3RD sing Verbs ith seith ath hath / e - sing. adj. / y]

TRANSLATION

Little Lewis, my son, I perceive well, because of certain evidence, your ability to learn sciences dealing with numbers and comparative relationships; and I consider as well your active
5 request especially to learn the story of the astrolabe. Then for as much as a philosopher says, "He wraps himself in his friend, who responds to the just requests of his friend," therefore I have given you an astrolabe suffi-
10 cient for our horizon, calibrated to the latitude of Oxford; upon which, through meditation on this little treatise, I intend to teach you (a) certain (number of) facts pertaining to the same instrument. I say "a certain number of facts"
15 for three reasons. The first reason is this: (you may) well believe that all the things that have been discovered or might possibly be discovered about so noble an instrument as an astrolabe are not perfectly known to any mortal man in
20 this region, it seems to me. Another reason is this, that truly in any treatise on the astrolabe I have seen, there are some assertions that will not always hold true; and some of them are too hard for your tender age of ten years to
25 understand.

I will show you this treatise, divided into five sections, with very easy rules and plain words in English, for you as yet know but little Latin, my little son. But, nevertheless, these reliable
30 matters are sufficient for you in English as well as these same matters suffice these noble Greek scholars in Greek; and Arabians in Arabic, and the Jews in Hebrew, and the Latin people in Latin, who first translated them out of several
35 other languages and wrote them in their own tongue, that is to say, in Latin. And God knows that in all these languages and in many more these matters have been sufficiently learned and taught, and yet by diverse rules; just as diverse
40 paths lead diverse people to Rome in the right way. Now I will meekly request every discreet person who reads or hears this little treatise to

EXERCISES

1. ME prose seems more like MnE than ME poetry does, although some differences remain. Compare the ME prose here and in the following selections to the MnE translations given, noting differences in word order and vocabulary.
2. How does the treatment of final unstressed –e differ here from its treatment in the preceding ME selections? Why? *[handwritten: not used - before for reasons of prosody]*
3. By ME times, the declension of the adjective has been greatly simplified. List the adjectives in this selection, noting whether they modify singular or plural nouns. What two inflectional forms do the *[handwritten: e]* singular adjectives have? (The syntactical reasons for the difference between these two categories of adjectives, strong and weak, need not concern us.) What inflectional form predominates in the plural? (Disyllables are uninflected.)
4. What forms does Chaucer use instead of the modern personal pronouns *their* and *them*? Does Chaucer use *they*? (All three forms are Scandinavian borrowings. Their use begins in the north and moves to the south.) Compare Chaucer's forms with the corresponding forms in OE. *[handwritten: her / thir / hem / they / pg. 66 l.26 / 16, 18]*
5. What two verbal endings for the third person singular does Chaucer use? (Consult the next selection as well.) Even though the two vowels are here transcribed differently, for purposes of consistency, how distinctly do you think the difference can be heard in unstressed syllables?
6. What ending does Chaucer use for the present participle? What ending is used in OE? *[handwritten: ende / yng]*
7. What is distinctive about Chaucer's use of the verb forms *be* and *been*? Also, compare their use in *The General Prologue* above.
8. Examine this and the other ME passages carefully to determine the forms of the ME personal pronoun, second person singular and plural, subjective and objective cases. What distinctions can ME writers make with this pronoun that we cannot? *[handwritten: sing + plu]*
9. Study the ME use of the relative pronouns *who*, *which*, *that*, and see what conclusions you can come to based on a comparison with MnE usage. *[handwritten: who, which, that]*

[handwritten notes at bottom: objective sing. the Pl. / thou / subj. thow ye / been - be? same / be - be? / that who / that that / whiche who / that who]

TEXT CONTINUED

cusid, and mȳ sūperfluitẹ of wordes, for twǭ causes. The first cause is for that curious
45 endītyng and hard sentence is ful hẹvy at ǭnys for such a chīld tǭ lẹrne. And the secunde cause is this, that sǭthly mẹ sẹmith better tǭ wrīten untǭ a chīld twȳes a gǭd sentence, than hẹ forgete it ǭnys.

TRANSCRIPTION CONTINUED

ɛndiːtɪŋg ɑnd hɑrd sɛntɛns ɪs fʊl hɛɪvɨ ɑt ɔɪnɪs fɔr sʊč ə čiːld toɪ leɪrn ɑnd θə sɛkʊnd kɑʊz ɪs θɪs θɑt soɪðlɨ meɪ seɪmɪθ bɛtɪər toɪ wriɪtən 45 ʊntoɪ ə čiːld twiɪəs ə goɪd sɛntɛns θɑn heɪ fɔrgɛt ɪt ɔɪnɪs]

TRANSLATION CONTINUED

excuse my simple writing, and my superfluity of words, for two reasons. The first reason is
45 that elaborate writing and difficult knowledge is at once very hard for such a child to learn. And the second reason is this, truly it seems to me better to write a good sentence twice for a child, than that he forget it once.

EXERCISES CONTINUED

10. Can you find a conjunction whose Chaucerian pronunciation survives dialectally into MnE?   (and)

11. The great extent to which French words contributed to the ME vocabulary is underscored by the fact that so many are found even in such a simple treatise, written for a young boy. How many readily identifiable French words can you find?

Geoffrey Chaucer

The Parson's Tale, 72–95

TEXT

Oure swẹẹte Lord God of hevene, that nǭ man
wole perisse, but wole that wẹ comen alle tǭ
the knǭweleche of hym, and tǭ the blisful līf
that is perdurāble, amonesteth us bȳ the proph-
5 ete Jeremie, that seith in thys wȳse: Stondeth
upon the weyes, and sẹẹth and axeth of ǭlde
pāthes (that is tǭ seyn, of ǭlde sentences) which
is the gọode wey, and walketh in that wey, and
yẹ shal fȳnde refresshynge for youre soules, etc.
10 Manye bẹẹn the weyes espirituels that lẹ̄den
folk tǭ oure Lǫrd Jhēsu Crīst, and tǭ the regne
of glǭrie. Of whiche weyes, thẹr is a ful nǭble
wey and a ful covenāble, which may nat fayle
tǭ man ne tǭ womman that thurgh synne hath
15 mysgọǭn frǭ the righte wey of Jerūsalem celestial; and this wey is clẹ̄ped Penitence, of which
man sholde gladly herknen and enquere with
al his herte, tǭ (wyten) what is Penitence, and
whennes it is clẹ̄ped Penitence, and in how
20 manye maneres bẹẹn the acciouns or werkynges
of Penitence, and how manye spẹ̄cẹ̄s thẹr bẹẹn
of Penitence, and whiche thynges apertẹ̄nen and
bihǭven tǭ Penitence, and whiche thynges
destourben Penitence.

     Seint Ambrǭse seith that Penitence is the
25 pleynynge of man for the gilt that hẹ hath
dǫon, and nāmǫǭre tǭ dǭ any thyng for which
hym oghte tǭ pleyne. And som doctour seith,
"Penitence is the waymentynge of man that
30 sorweth for his synne, and pȳneth hymself for
hẹ hath mysdǫon." Penitence, with certeyne
circumstances, is verray repentance of a man
that halt hymself in sorwe and ọother peyne
for his giltes. And for hẹ shal bẹ verray peni-
35 tent, hẹ shal first biwaylen the synnes that hẹ
hath dǫon, and stidefastly purposen in his herte
tǭ have shrift of mouthe, and tǭ dǫon satisfac-
cioun, and nevere tǭ dǫon thyng for which
hym oghte mǭore tǭ biwayle or tǭ compleyne,
40 and tǭ continue in gǫode werkes, or elles his
repentance may nat availle.

TRANSCRIPTION

[uːr sweɪt lɔrd gɔd ɔf hɛvən θɑt nɔː mɑn wɔl
pɛrɪš bʊt wɔl θɑt weː kʊmən ɑl toː θə knɔːwəlɛʝ
ɔf hɪm ɑnd toː θə blɪsfʊl liːf θɑt ɪs pɛrdʊrɑːblə
ɑmɔnɛstəθ ʊs biː θə prɔfɛt ˈʝɛrɛmɪ θɑt sæːθ ɪn
5 θɪs wiːz stɔndəθ ʊpɔn θə wæːɪəs ɑnd seːθ ɑnd
ɑksəθ ɔf ɔːld pɑːðəs θɑt ɪs toː sæːn ɔf ɔːld sɛn-
tɛnsəs hwɪč ɪs θə gɔːd wæː ɑnd wɑlkəθ ɪn θɑt
wæː ɑnd jeː šɑl fiːnd rɛfrɛšɪŋg fɔr juːr suːləs
mɑnɪ beːn θə wæːɪəs ɛspɪrɪtʊɛls θɑt lɛːɪdən fɔlk
toː uːr lɔːrd ˈjeːsʊ kriːst ɑnd toː θə ræːn ɔf glɔːrɪ
10 ɔf hwɪč wæːɪəs θɛːr ɪs ə fʊl nɔːblə wæː ɑnd ə fʊl
kɔvenɑːblə hwɪč mæː nɑt fæːl toː mɑn nə toː
wɔmːɑn θɑt θʊrx sɪn hɑθ mɪsgɔːn frɔː θə rɪxt
wæː ɔf ˈʝeruːsɑlɛm sɛlɛstɪɑl ɑnd θɪs wæː ɪs klɛːɪpəd
pɛnɪtɛns ɔf hwɪč mɑn šɔld glɑdlɪ hɛrknən ɑnd
15 ɛnkwɛr wɪθ ɑl ɪs hɛrt toː wɪtən hwɑt ɪs pɛnɪtɛns ɑnd hwɛnːəs ɪt ɪs klɛːɪpəd pɛnɪtɛns ɑnd ɪn
huː mɑnɪ mɑnɛrəs beːn θə akɪsɪuːns ɔr wɛrkɪŋgəs
ɔf pɛnɪtɛns ɑnd huː mɑnɪ speːseːs θɛːr beːn ɔf
pɛnɪtɛns ɑnd hwɪč θɪŋgəs ɑpɛrtɛːnən ɑnd
20 bɪhɔːvən toː pɛnɪtɛns ɑnd hwɪč θɪŋgəs dɛs-
tuːrbən pɛnɪtɛns

    sæːnt ɑmbrɔːz sæːθ θɑt pɛnɪtɛns ɪs θə plæːnɪŋg
ɔf mɑn fɔr θə gɪlt θɑt heː ɑθ doːn ɑnd nɑːmɔːr
toː doː ɑnɪ θɪŋg fɔr hwɪč ɪm ɔuxt toː plæːn
25 ɑnd sʊm dɔktuːr sæːθ pɛnɪtɛns ɪs θə wæːmɛntɪŋg
ɔf mɑn θɑt sɔrwəθ fɔr ɪs sɪn ɑnd piːnəθ ɪmsɛlf
fɔr heː ɑθ mɪsdoːn pɛnɪtɛns wɪθ sɛrtæːn
sɪrkʊmstɑnsəs ɪs vɛrːæː rɛpɛntɑnts ɔf ə mɑn
θɑt hɑlt ɪmsɛlf ɪn sɔrwə ɑnd ɔːðər pæːn fɔr
30 ɪs gɪltəs ɑnd fɔr eː šɑl beː vɛrːæː pɛnɪtɛnt heː
šɑl fɪrst bɪwæːlən θə sɪnːəs θɑt heː hɑθ doːn
ɑnd stɪdefɑstlɪ pʊrpɔsən ɪn ɪs hɛrt toː hɑv
šrɪft ɔf muːθ ɑnd toː doːn sɑtɪsfɑksɪuːn ɑnd
nɛvər toː doːn θɪŋg fɔr hwɪč ɪm ɔuxt mɔːr
35 toː bɪwæːl ɔr toː kɔmplæːn ɑnd toː kɔntɪnɪʊ
ɪn gɔːd wɛrkəs ɔr ɛlːəs hɪs rɛpɛntɑnts mæː
nɑt ɑvæːl]

TRANSLATION

Our sweet Lord God of heaven, who wishes no
man to perish, but wishes that we all (may)
come to the knowledge of Him, and to the blissful life that is eternal, admonishes us by the
prophet Jeremiah, who says in this manner:
"Stand upon the roads, and see and ask about
old paths (that is to say, about old meanings)
which is the good road, and walk on that road,
and you shall find refreshment for your souls,"
etc. Many are the spiritual roads that lead
folk to our Lord Jesus Christ, and to the kingdom of glory. Concerning which roads, there
is a very noble and suitable road, which may
not fail (a) man or woman who by means of
sin has strayed from the right road toward
celestial Jerusalem; and this road is called
Penitence, to which man should gladly pay
attention and inquire (about) with all his heart,
to learn what Penitence is, and why it is called
Penitence, and in how many ways are the
actions or workings of Penitence, and how many
species there are of Penitence, and which things
appertain and are necessary to Penitence, and
which things disturb Penitence.

Saint Ambrose says that Penitence is the
lamenting of man for the sin he has done, and
concerning which he will no more do anything
to lament for. And a certain doctor (of the
church) says, "Penitence is the lament of man
who sorrows on account of his sin, and tortures
himself because he has done wrong." Penitence,
under certain circumstances, is (the) true repentance of a man who holds himself in sorrow
and other pain because of his sins. And for him
to be truly penitent, he shall first bewail the
sins he has committed, and steadfastly determine in his heart to confess with his mouth,
and perform penance satisfactorily, and never
to do anything for which he ought to be sorry
or to lament, and to continue in good works, or
else his repentance cannot help him.

EXERCISES

1. What is distinctive about the syntactical pattern
in lines 12–13, where two adjectives modify the same
noun? Is this construction in use in MnE? (It is
quite common in OE.) What is distinctive about the
position of the adjective in line 10 and again in
lines 15–16? Is this word order used in OE? (Check
an OE prose selection.) Under what circumstances
is it used in MnE? Are the adjectives here native
words or borrowed? Does this suggest another reason
for the word order here?

2. Notice the root vowels in *comen* (2) and *stondeth*
(5). Look up the etymology of these native words.
The *o* in *comen* (like the *o* in MnE *honey*, *love*,
wonder, *monk*, and *tongue*) is a purely orthographic
device introduced about the twelfth century by
scribes to make the letter following it easier to discern. In OE, the short mid-back vowel and the short
low-back vowel often alternate before nasals.

3. What is the origin of *frǫ* (15)? Does Chaucer use
from as well? Under what circumstance is *fro* used
in MnE?

4. Look up the etymology of *admonish* and compare Chaucer's form (4). From what language is
the modern *d* taken? This intrusive letter is added
in the English Renaissance period by pedants. Is
the *d* reflected phonologically? (Cf. ME *āventure*,
dette, *doute*.)

5. The *r* sound has caused peculiar sound changes
in the history of English. Note the Chaucerian pronunciation of the following words: *werkes* (40) and
werkynges (20), *herte* (18), *herknen* (17), *first* (35),
and *destourben* (24). Compare these pronunciations
with their modern pronunciations. In ME, which of
the vowels before –*r* are identical in sound? which in
MnE? How have the spellings changed in each
instance? Can you think of possible similar developments in other words? (Check your suppositions in
Webster's Third or in the *OED*.)

6. How does the occurrence of the word *refresshynge*
(9) show how extensive the borrowing of French

EXERCISES CONTINUED

words is in late ME? (Hint: what is the origin of the
–ynge ending?) Cf. *werkynges* (20).

7. What is the pronunciation of *axeth* (6) and *thurgh*
(14)? Look up the etymology of these words. How
do you account phonologically for ME *ax–* becoming
MnE *ask*? (See a dictionary for the meaning of the
term "metathesis.") Does this ME pronunciation
also survive into MnE? Similarly, why does ME
thurgh become MnE *through*? (What is the etymology
of MnE *thorough*?)

8. What is distinctive about the ME pronunciation
of *alle* (2) or *al* (18) in comparison to the MnE
pronunciation?

9. Account for the *–en* endings of *biwaylen* (35) and
purposen (36).

10. What common OE verbal prefix occurs in lines
15 and 31? What meaning does it have in these
two words? To what extent is the negating prefix
still viable in MnE?

11. At the very end of the ME period, *–e–* in an
unstressed final syllable is very often lost altogether.
What effect does this sound change have on the
following words: *whennes* (19), *clēped* (19), *elles*
(40)? In the case of *clēped*, what concomitantly
happens to the final *–d*? Why? (Is the *–þ–* voiced
or voiceless?) This last sound change is called
"assimilation."

The Lord's Prayer

(*Matthew* 6: 9–13)

TEXT

Oure fadir
that art in heuenes,
halewid bē thī nāme;
4 thī kyngdǫǫm come tǭ;
bē thī wille dǫn in ērthe as in heuene;
ʒyue tǭ vs this dai oure brēęd ǭuer ǭthir
    substaunce;
and forʒyue tǭ vs oure dettis, as wē forʒyuen
    tǭ oure dettouris;
8 and lēde vs not in tǭ temptācioun,
but dēlyuere vs frǭ ȳuel. Amēn.

TRANSCRIPTION

[uːr fɑdɪr
θɑt ɑrt ɪn hɛvɛnəs
hɑləwɪd beː θiː nɑːm
4 θiː kɪŋdoːm kʊm toː
beː θiː wɪl doːn ɪn eːrθ ɑs ɪn hɛvən
gɪv toː ʊs θɪs dæɪ uːr brɛɪd ɔːvər oːðɪr sʊbstɑʊns
ɑnd fɔrgɪv toː ʊs uːr dɛtɪɪs ɑs weː fɔrgɪvən toː
    uːr dɛtɪʊːrɪs
8 ɑnd lɛɪd ʊs nɔt ɪn toː tɛmptɑːsɪuːn
bʊt deːlɪvər ʊs frɔː iːvɛl ɑmɛɪn]

(handwritten margin notes: — þū þe → that; loss of inflectional endings to indicate dat.; Dat. P. → es, um → e, eo → u(v), f → u(v))

EXERCISES

1. Compare in detail this passage with the same OE prayer. List specific differences in word order, morphology, spelling, and pronunciation.

2. In comparing the two prayers, what change do you note in the use of the relative pronoun in line 2?

3. Find instances of the increased use of the preposition in ME. How do you account for this phenomenon?

4. Is the subjunctive still apparent in the ME prayer? (Cf. the OE usage.) Is the distinction made between singular and plural verb forms? *(handwritten: e en)*

5. What is the inflected form of the plural verb in line 7? How does it differ from the MnE form it develops into? What would the OE plural form *–aþ* *(handwritten: with eth)* normally have become in ME? What singular form would it consequently have been confused with? (The ME *–e(n)* developed probably by analogy with the OE subjunctive ending. Note: the present-day English *singular* form in *–s* develops not from the Midland *–eth* form, but from the Northern form in

(handwritten margin: p. 27)

–(e)s. Chaucer's *–eth* does not survive much beyond the EMnE period.)

6. How many of the several orthographical and morphological changes from OE *heofonum* to ME *heuenes* can you account for?

7. Notice the development of OE *ūs* [uːs] into ME *ŭs* [ʊs] (6) into MnE [ʌs]. Is this development of OE *ū* regular? (Refer to the vowel chart, p. 33.) Cf. the similar development of OE *būton* [–uː–], which > ME *bŭt* [–ʊ–] (9) > MnE *but* [–ʌ–]. (In the OE prayer, an alternate form *ac* is used, which does not survive at all.)

8. In the two prayers, what OE word is replaced by ME *brēęd*? With what form and meaning has the OE word survived into MnE? (The semantic change involved is called "specialization.")

9. How many OE words are replaced in the ME prayer with other words? How many of the new words are foreign borrowings? Have these survived into MnE?

(handwritten margin right: hlāf (loaf) ā → [oː])

(handwritten bottom: hath or have)

The Prodigal Son

(Luke 15: 11–32)

TEXT

And hē seide, A man hadde twei sones; and the
ȝonger of hem seide tō the fadir, Fadir, ȝyue
mē the porcioun of catel, that fallith tō mē. And
hē departide tō hem the catel.

5 And not aftir many daies, whanne alle thingis
wēren gederid tōgider, the ȝonger sone wente
forth in pilgrymāge in tō a fer cuntrē; and thēre
hē wastide hise goọdis in lyuynge lecherously.
And aftir that hē hadde endid alle thingis, a
10 strong hungre was maad in that cuntrē, and
hē began tō haue nēde. And hē wente, and drouȝ
hym tō ọọn of the citeseyns of that cuntrē.
And hē sente hym in tō his toun, tō fēde swȳn.
And hē coueitide tō fille his wombe of the coddis
15 that the hoggis ẹẹten, and nọ man ȝaf hym.

And hē turnede aȝen tō hym silf, and seide,
Hou many hīrid men in mȳ ⟨fadir⟩ hous han
plentē of loọues; and Ȳ perische here thorouȝ
hungir. Ȳ schal rīse vp, and gọ tō mȳ fadir,
20 and Ȳ schal seie tō hym, Fadir, Ȳ haue synned
in tō heuene, and bifor thẹẹ; and now Ȳ am
not worthi tō bē clẹpid thī sone, māke mē as
ọọn of thīn hīrid men.

And hē rọọs vp, and cam tō his fadir. And
25 whanne hē was ȝit afer, his fadir saiȝ hym,
and was stirrid bī mercy. And hē ran, and fel
on his necke, and kisside hym. And the sone
seide tō hym, Fadir, Ȳ haue synned in tō heuene,
and bifor thẹẹ; and now Ȳ am not worthi tō
30 bē clẹpid thī sone.

And the fadir seide tō hise seruauntis, Swīthe
brynge ȝē forth the firste stoọle, and clọthe ȝē
hym, and ȝyue ȝē a ryng iṅ his hoond, and
schoọn on hise fẹẹt; and brynge ȝē a fat calf,
35 and slē ȝē, and ẹte wē, and māke wē fẹẹste.
For this mȳ sone was dẹẹd, and hath lyued
aȝen; hē perischid, and is foundun. And alle
men bigunnen tō ẹte.

But his eldere sone was in the fẹẹld; and
40 whanne hē cam, and neiȝede tō the hous, hē
herde a symfonȳe and a croude. And hē clẹpide

TRANSCRIPTION

[ɑnd heː sæɪd ə mɑn hɑd ˈtwæɪ sʊnəs ɑnd θə
jʊŋgər ɔf hɛm sæɪd tɔː θə fɑdɪr fɑdɪr jɪv meː
θə pɔrsɪuːn ɔf kɑtəl θɑt fɑlːɪθ tɔː meː ɑnd heː
dɛpɑrtɪd tɔː hɛm θə kɑtəl

ɑnd nɔt ɑftɪr mɑnɪ dæɪəs hwɑn ɑl θɪŋgɪs 5
wæɪrən gɛdɪrɪd tɔːgɪdər θə jʊŋgər sʊn wɛnt
fɔrθ ɪn pɪlgrɪmɑːĭ ɪn tɔː ə fɛr kʊntreː ɑnd θɛɪr
heː wɑstɪd hɪz gɔːdɪs ɪn lɪvɪŋ lɛčəruːslɪ ɑnd
ɑftɪr θɑt heː hɑd ɛndɪd ɑl θɪŋgəs ə strɔŋg hʊŋgrə
wɑs mɑɪd ɪn θɑt kʊntreː ɑnd heː bɛgɑn tɔː 10
hɑv neːd ɑnd heː wɛnt ɑnd druːx ɪm tɔː ɔːn
ɔf θə sɪtəsæɪns ɔf θɑt kʊntreː ɑnd heː sɛnt ɪm
ɪn tɔː ɪs tuːn tɔː feːd swiːn ɑnd heː kɔvæɪtɪd
tɔː fɪl ɪs wɔmb ɔf θə kɔdɪːs θɑt θə hɔgɪːs ɛɪtən
ɑnd nɔː mɑn jɑf ɪm 15

ɑnd heː tʊrnəd ajɛn tɔː hɪm sɪlf ɑnd sæɪd huɪ
mɑnɪ hiːrɪd mɛn ɪn miː fɑdɪr huːs hɑn plɛnteː
ɔf lɔɪvəs ɑnd iː pɛrɪš hɛr θɔruːx hʊŋgɪr iː šɑl
riːz up ɑnd gɔː tɔː miː fɑdɪr ɑnd iː šɑl sæɪ tɔː
hɪm fɑdɪr iː hɑv sɪnːəd ɪn tɔː hɛvɛn ɑnd bɪfɔr 20
θeː ɑnd nuː iː ɑm nɔt wʊrðɪ tɔː biː klɛɪpɪd θiː
sʊn mɑɪk meː ɑs ɔːn ɔf θiːn hiːrɪd mɛn

ɑnd heː rɔːs up ɑnd kɑm tɔː ɪs fɑdɪr ɑnd
hwɑn heː wɑs jɪt ɑfɛr ɪs fɑdɪr sæɪx ɪm ɑnd wɑs
stɪrːɪd biː mɛrsɪ ɑnd heː rɑn ɑnd fɛl ɔn ɪs nɛk 25
ɑnd kɪsːɪd ɪm ɑnd θə sʊn sæɪd tɔː ɪm fɑdɪr iː
hɑv sɪnːəd ɪn tɔː hɛvən ɑnd bɪfɔr θeː ɑnd nuː
iː ɑm nɔt wʊrðɪ tɔː beː klɛɪpɪd θiː sʊn

ɑnd θə fɑdɪr sæɪd tɔː ɪz sɛrvɑuntɪs swɪːðə
brɪŋg jeː fɔrθ θə fɪrst stɔːl ɑnd klɔːð jeː hɪm 30
ɑnd jɪv jeː ə rɪŋg ɪn ɪs hɔnd ɑnd šoːn ɔn ɪz
feːt ɑnd brɪŋg jeː ə fɑt kɑlf ɑnd sleː jeː ɑnd
ɛɪt weː ɑnd mɑɪk weː fɛɪst fɔr θɪs miː sʊn wɑs
dɛɪd ɑnd ɑθ lɪvəd ajɛn heː pɛrɪšɪd ɑnd ɪs
fuːndʊn ɑnd ɑl mɛn bɪgʊnɪən tɔː ɛɪt 35

bʊt ɪs ɛldər sʊn wɑs ɪn θə feːld ɑnd hwɑn
eː kɑm ɑnd næɪjəd tɔː θə huːs heː hɛrd ə
sɪmfɔnɪə ɑnd ə kruːd ɑnd eː klɛɪpɪd ɔːn ɔf θə
sɛrvɑuntɪs ɑnd ɑksɪd hwɑt θɛɪz θɪŋgɪs wæɪrən
ɑnd eː sæɪd tɔː ɪm θiː brɔːðər ɪs kʊmʊn ɑnd 40
θiː fɑdɪr slɛʊ ə fɑt kɑlf fɔr heː rɛsɪæɪvəd ɪm

TEXT CONTINUED

ǫǫn of the seruauntis, and axide, what thẹse
thingis wẹren. And hẹ seide tǭ hym, Thī brǭther
is comun, and thī fadir slewe a fat calf, for hẹ
45 resseyuede hym saaf. And hẹ was wrǫǫth, and
wolde not come in. Thẹrfor his fadir wente out,
and bigan tǭ preye hym.

And hẹ answerde tǭ his fadir, and seide, Lǭ!
sǭ many ȝẹẹris Ȳ serue thẹẹ, and Ȳ neuer brak
50 thī comaundement; and thou neuer ȝaf tǭ mẹ
a kidde, that Ȳ with mȳ frẹẹndis schulde haue
ẹte. But aftir that this thī sone, that hath
deuourid his substaunce with hǭris, cam, thou
hast slayn tǭ hym a fat calf. And hẹ seide tǭ
55 hym, Sone, thou art euer mǭre with mẹ, and
alle mȳ thingis bẹn thīne. But it bihǫfte for tǭ
māke fẹẹste, and tǭ haue ioye; for this thī
brǭther was dẹẹd, and lyuede aȝen; hẹ perischide,
and is foundun.

TRANSCRIPTION CONTINUED

sɑːf ɑnd heː wɑs wrɔːθ ɑnd wɔld nɔt kʊm ɪn
θɛːrfɔr ɪs fɑdɪr wɛnt uːt ɑnd bɪgɑn toː præi ɪm
ɑnd heː ɑnswɛrd toː ɪs fɑdɪr ɑnd sæid lɔː sɔː
mɑnɪ jɛːrɪs iː sɛrv θeː ɑnd iː nɛvər brɑk θiː 45
kɔmɑʊndəmənt ɑnd θuː nɛvər jɑf toː meː ə kɪd
θɑt iː wɪθ miː freɪndɪs ʃʊld hɑv ɛːt bʊt ɑftɪr
θɑt θɪs θiː sʊn θɑt hɑθ dɛvuːrɪd ɪs sʊbstɑʊns
wɪθ hɔːrɪs kɑm θuː hɑst slæin toː hɪm ə fɑt
kɑlf ɑnd heː sæid toː ɪm sʊn θuː ɑrt ɛvər mɔːr 50
wɪθ meː ɑnd ɑl miː θɪŋgɪs beːn θiːn bʊt ɪt
bɪhɔːft fɔr toː mɑːk fɛːst ɑnd toː hɑv jɔi fɔr
θɪs θiː brɔːðər wɑs dɛːd ɑnd lɪvəd ɑjɛn heː
pɛrɪʃɪd ɑnd ɪs fuːndʊn]

EXERCISES

1. Compare in detail this extended prose passage with the corresponding OE selection, listing specific differences in word order, morphology, spelling, and pronunciation, coming to whatever general conclusions you can.

2. Also note in each of the above instances the specific differences between ME and MnE practice and draw appropriate conclusions.

3. How many of the OE words have been replaced by other words? How many of them are French borrowings? Have these survived into MnE?

4. Comparing the two versions, notice the following changes in meaning or form from OE times to ME times. Line references are to the ME passage.

OE *syle* 'give' > MnE *sell*; beside ME *ȝyue* (2)

OE *dǣl*; ME *porcioun* (3). Does the OE word survive into MnE? In what phrases?

OE *þing*; ME *thingis* (5). The OE unchanged plural is regularized in ME.

OE *forspilde*; ME *wastide* (8). Notice the OE intensifying prefix and the subsequent specialization of the root.

OE *burhsittendan* 'the burg sitters'; ME *citeseyns* (12). Compare MnE *borough*.

OE *ic ārīse*; ME *Ȳ schal rīse vp* (19). Note the mandatory use of the auxiliary in ME.

5. Comment on the following changes in meaning or form from ME times to MnE times:

ME *departide* (4) *given abroad*
ME *pilgrymāge* (7)
ME *aftir that* (9) *when*
ME *hungre* (10) *famine*
ME *hym* (12). The reflexive is sometimes used in MnE, especially colloquially.
ME *wombe* (14) *stomach*
ME *hym* (15); but cf. *tǭ hym* (20)
in mȳ fadir hous (17). Derived from the similar OE construction: the genitive of nouns of relationship is uninflected.
ME *afer* (25). Survives dialectally.
ME *schǫǫn* (34). Declined like OE weak nouns.

6. Although neither in ME nor in MnE has the distinction in the spelling of long and short vowels been consistent, ME scribes tend to double long vowels in closed syllables (i.e., syllables ending in a consonant). Find examples.

7. What phonetic values does the letter ȝ have in this selection? (It is sometimes impossible to be sure which sound the scribe intends to represent.) [j] [x]

8. Can you account for the two pronunciations of the word for "his" in line 31 of the phonetic transcription?

[ɪs] his
[ɪz] hise

Sir Gawain and the Green Knight, 516–535

TEXT

After þe sęsoun of somer wyth þe soft wyndez
Quen Zeferus syflez hymself on sędez and erbez,
Węla wynne is þe wort þat waxes þeroute,
When þe donkande dęwe dropez of þe lęuez,
5   Tǫ bīde a blysful blusch of þe bryȝt sunne.
Bot þen hȳȝes heruest, and hardenes hym sǫne,
Warnez hym for þe wynter tǫ wax ful rȳpe;
Hę drȳues wyth droȝt þe dust for tǫ rȳse,
Frǫ þe fāce of þe fǫlde tǫ flȳȝe ful hȳȝe;
10   Wrǫþe wynde of þe welkyn wrastelez with þe
        sunne,
      þe lęuez lancen frǫ þe lynde and lyȝten on þe
        grounde,
      And al grayes þe gres þat gręne watz ęre;
      Þenne al rȳpez and rǫtez þat rǫs vpon fyrst,
      And þus ȝirnez þe ȝęre in ȝisterdayez mony,
15   And wynter wyndez aȝayn, as þe worlde askez,
        nǫ fāge,
        Til Meȝelmas mǫne
        Watz cumen wyth wynter wāge;
        Þen þenkkez Gāwan ful sǫne
20   Of his anious uyāge.

TRANSCRIPTION

[aftər θə sɛɪzuːn ɔf sʊmər wɪθ θə sɔft wɪndəs
hwɛn zɛfɛrʊs sɪfləs ɪmsɛlf ɔn seɪdəs and ɛrbəs
wɛɪla wɪn ɪs θə wɔrt θat waksəs θɛruːtə
hwɛn θə dɔnkandə dɛʊə drɔpəs ɔf θə lɛɪvəs
·tɔː bɪːd ə blɪsfʊl blʊš ɔf θə brɪxt sʊnɪə   5
bʊt θɛn hɪːxəs hɛrvɛst and hardənəs ɪm sɔɪnə
warnəs hɪm fɔr θə wɪntɛr tɔː waks fʊl rɪːpə
heɪ drɪːvəs wɪθ drʊxt θə dʊst fɔr tɔː rɪːzə
frɔː θə faɪs ɔf θə fɔɪldə tɔː flɪːxə fʊl hɪːxə
wrɔɪðə wɪnd ɔf θə wɛlkɪn wrastələs wɪθ θə sʊnɪə   10
θə lɛɪvəs lansən frɔː θə lɪnd and lɪxtən ɔn θə
        gruɪndə
and al græɪəs θə grɛs θat greɪnə was ɛɪrə
θɛn al rɪːpəs and rɔɪtəs θat rɔɪs ʊpɔn fɪrst
and θʊs jɪrnəs θə jɛɪr ɪn jɪstɛrdæɪəs mɔnɪ
and wɪntɛr wɪndəs aʒæɪn as θə wɔrld askəs   15
        nɔɪ faɪʒə
        tɪl mɛxɛlmas mɔɪnə
        was kʊmən wɪθ wɪntɛr waɪʒə
        θɛn θɛnkɪəs gaɪwan fʊl sɔɪnə
        ɔf ɪs anɪuɪs vɪaɪʒə]   20

86

TRANSLATION

After the season of summer with the soft winds
When Zephyrus blows himself on seeds and
    herbs,
Very joyful is the plant that grows thereout,
When the dripping dew drops from the leaves,
5 To await a blissful blush from the bright sun.
But then harvest hastens; and encourages him
    at once,
Warns him on account of the winter to grow
    fully ripe;
He drives against the drought to raise the dust,
From the face of the earth to fly very high;
10 Angry wind from the sky wrestles with the sun,
The leaves fly from the limetree and alight on
    the ground,
And all gray (is) the grass that was green before;
Then all ripens and rots that rose at the first,
And thus passes the year in yesterdays many,
15 And winter returns again, as the world demands,
    without a doubt,
    Till Michaelmas moon
    Has come with winter challenge;
    Then Gawain thinks very soon
20   Of his troublesome voyage.

whimsical
whinsome

6 + 19

EXERCISES

1. Assuming that syllables are, relative to one another, either stressed or unstressed, scan several lines from the passage and compare them metrically with several lines from *Beowulf* or another OE poem. What differences do you note? How are they to be accounted for? Note particularly the number of stressed syllables in each line of the ME poem and compare with OE practice.

2. Does the use of alliteration seem to affect the word order?

3. How many alliterative sounds occur in a single line? Is the number the same in every line? Which stressed syllable in each line is not alliterated?

4. Compare the use of alliteration here with that in *Beowulf*. What differences are noticeable?

5. Why is it impossible for a modern translation to be close metrically to a ME poem?

6. Why is it nearly impossible, if not in fact so, for the alliterative pattern to be maintained in a modern translation?

7. Does the same alliterating sound ever extend beyond the bounds of a single line? (The same alliterating sound sometimes dominates several lines in succession elsewhere in the poem.)

8. Does the last word of a line ever establish the alliterating sound for the next?

9. Do the lines tend to be end-stopped, or do the phrases usually run over to the following line?

10. Does the last word in each line seem as important as it does in much modern poetry? Give reasons for your answer.

11. Does ME *wort* (3) survive into MnE as a word? As a combining element?

12. What does *wynne* (3) mean? Can you think of a MnE word that contains it?

13. Find an example of *soon* in the passage with its old meaning and another example with its modern meaning. What conclusion can you come to if both meanings exist side by side in ME?

14. What peculiar spellings do you find in this selection as compared to the preceding ME selections?

15. *Gawain* is written in the Northwest Midland region, so that we can expect Northern as well as Midland dialect features. List examples of the Northern features (see p. 27), and compare them with Chaucer's Southeast Midland features. Do you find any West Midland features?

Middle English Lyrics

TEXT	TRANSCRIPTION

Sumer is i-cumen in

Sing, cuccu, nū! Sing, cuccu!
Sing, cuccu! Sing, cuccu, nū!

Sumer is i-cumen in;
   Lhūde sing, cuccu!
5 Grǭweþ sēd, and blǭweþ mēd,
   And springþ þe w⟨u⟩de nū.
    Sing cuccu!
Awe blēteþ after lomb,
   Lhouþ after calve cū;
10 Bulluc sterteþ, bucke verteþ;
   Murie sing, cuccu!
    Cuccu! cuccu!
  Wēl singes þū, cuccu;
   Ne swik þū naver nū.

Sumer is i-cumen in

[sɪŋg kʊkɪʊ nuː sɪŋg kʊkɪʊ
sɪŋg kʊkɪʊ sɪŋg kʊkɪʊ nuː

sʊmər ɪs ɨkʊmən ɪn
luːdə sɪŋg kʊkɪʊ
grɔːwəθ seːd ɑnd blɔːwəθ meːd   5
ɑnd sprɪŋgθ θə wʊdə nuː
sɪŋg kʊkɪʊ
ɑwə blɛɪtəθ ɑftər lɔmb
luːθ ɑftər kɑlvə kuː
bʊlːʊk stɛrtəθ bʊkə vɛrtəθ   10
mʊrɨ sɪŋg kʊkɪʊ
kʊkɪʊ kʊkɪʊ
weːl sɪŋgəs θuː kʊkɪʊ
nɛ swɪk θuː nɑvər nuː]

Nuo goth sonne under wode

Nou gǭth sonne under wǭde;
Mē rewes, Marie, þī faire rǭde.
Nou gǭth sonne under trē;
Mē rewes, Marie, þī sone and þē.

Nou goth sonne under wode

[nuː gɔːθ sʊn ʊnder woːdə
meː rɛʊəs mɑrɨ θiː fæɪrə roːdə
nuː gɔːθ sʊn ʊndər treː
meː rɛʊəs mɑrɨ θiː sʊn ɑnd θeː]

TRANSLATION

Sumer is i-cumen in

Sing, cuckoo, now! Sing, cuckoo!
Sing, cuckoo! Sing, cuckoo, now!

Spring has come in;
   Loudly sing, cuckoo!
5 Seed grows, and meadow blooms,
   And the wood grows now.
     Sing cuckoo!
Ewe bleats after lamb,
   Cow lows after calf;
10 Bullock jumps, buck farts;
   Merry sing, cuckoo!
     Cuckoo! Cuckoo!
Sing you well, cuckoo;
Nor stop you never now.

Nou goth sonne under wode

Now goes sun under wood;
I have sorrow, Mary, for thy fair face.
Now goes sun under tree;
I have sorrow, Mary, for thy son and thee.

TEXT CONTINUED

When the nyhtegale singes

When þe nyhtegāle singes,
   þe wǭdes waxen grēne;
Lēf ant gras ant blosme springes
   In Averyl, ȳ wēne;
5 Ant love is tǭ mȳn herte gǭn
   Wiþ ǭne spēre sǭ kēne,
Nyht ant day mȳ blǭd hit drynkes,
   Mȳn herte dēþ mē tēne.

Ich have loved al þis ჳēr,
10   þat ȳ may love nā mǭre;
Ich have siked moni syk,
   Lemmon, for þīn ǭre;
Mē nis love never þe nēr,
   Ant þat mē reweþ sǭre;
15 Suēte lemmon; þench on mē,
   Ich have loved þē ჳōre.

Suēte lemmon, ȳ preye þē
   Of love ǭne spēche;
Whīl ȳ lyve in world sǭ wȳde
20   Ǭþer nulle ȳ sēche.
Wiþ þȳ love, mȳ suēte leof,
   Mȳ blis þou mihtes ēche;
A suēte cos of þȳ mouþ
   Mihte bē mȳ lēche.

25 Suēte lemmon, ȳ preჳe þē
   Of a love-bēne:
ჳef þou mē lovest, ase men says,
   Lemmon, as ȳ wēne,
Ant ჳef hit þī wille bē,
30   þou lǭke þat hit bē sēne;
Sǭ muchel ȳ þenke upon þē
   þat al ȳ waxe grēne.

Bituēne Lyncolne ant Lyndeseye,
   Norhamptoun ant Lounde,
35 Ne wǭt ȳ non sǭ fayr a may,
   As ȳ gǭ fore y-bounde.
Suēte lemmon, ȳ preჳe þē
   þou lovie mē a stounde;
Ȳ wole mone mȳ song
40   On wham þat hit ys on y-long.

TRANSCRIPTION CONTINUED

When the nyhtegale singes

[hwɛn θə nɪxtəgɑːlə sɪŋgəs
θə woːdəs waksən greːnə
lɛːf ɑnd grɑs ɑnd blɔsmə sprɪŋgəs
ɪn ɑvərɪl iː weːnə
ɑnd lʊv ɪs toː miːn hɛrtə gɔːn   5
wɪθ ɔːnə spɛːrə sɔː keːnə
nɪxt ɑnd dæɪ miː blɔːd hɪt drɪŋkəs
miːn hɛrtə deːθ meː teːnə

ɪč hɑvə lʊvəd ɑl θɪs jɛːr
θɑt iː mæɪ lʊv nɑː mɔːrə   10
ɪč hɑvə sɪkəd mɔnɪ sɪk
lemiːn fɔr θiːn ɔːrə
meː nɪs lʊvə nɛvər θə nɛːr
ɑnd θɑt meː rɛʊəθ sɔːrə
sweːtə lemiːn θɛnč ɔn meː   15
ɪč hɑvə lʊvəd θeː jɔːrə

sweːtə lemiːn iː præɪə θeː
ɔf lʊv ɔːnə speːčə
hwiːl iː lɪv ɪn wɔrld sɔː wiːdə
oːðər nʊl iː seːčə   20
wɪθ θiː lʊvə miː sweːtə lɛɔf
miː blɪs θuː mɪxtəs eːčə
ə sweːtə kɔs ɔf θiː muːθ
mɪxtə beː miː leːčə

sweːtə lemiːn iː præɪə θeː   25
ɔf ə lʊvəbeːnə
jɛf θuː meː lʊvəst ɑs mɛn sæɪs
lemiːn ɑs iː weːnə
ɑnd jɛf hɪt θiː wɪlə beː
θuː loːkə θɑt hɪt beː seːnə   30
sɔː mʊčəl iː θɛŋk ʊpɔn θeː
θɑt ɑl iː waksə greːnə

bɪtweːnə lɪŋkɔln ɑnd lɪndəzæɪə
nɔrhamptuːn ɑnd luːndə
nə wɔːt iː nɔn sɔː fæɪr ə mæɪ   35
ɑs iː gɔː fɔr ɬbuːndə
sweːtə lemiːn iː præɪə θeː
θuː lʊvə meː ə stuːndə
iː wɔlə mʊn miː sɔŋg
ɔn hwɑm θɑt hɪt ɪs ɔn ɬɔŋg]   40

TRANSLATION CONTINUED

When the nightegale singes

When the nightingale sings,
   The woods wax green;
Leaf and grass and blossom grow
   In April, I believe;
5 And love has gone to my heart
   With one spear so keen,
Night and day my blood it drinks,
   My heart does trouble me.

I have loved all this year,
10   So that I can love no more;
I have sighed many (a) sigh,
   Sweetheart, for your mercy;
Love is never the nearer to me,
   And that sorrows me sorely;
15 Sweet lady; think on me,
   I have loved you long.

Sweet lady, I pray you
   One speech of love;
While I live in (the) world so wide
20   Another I will not seek.
With thy love, my sweet beloved,
   You might augment my bliss;
A sweet kiss from thy mouth
   Would be my doctor.

25 Sweet lady, I pray you
   For a lover's petition:
If you love me, as men say,
   Lady, as I hope,
And if it is thy will,
30   Look thou that it be evident;
I think upon you so much
   That I become entirely pale.

Between Lincoln and Lindsey,
   Northampton and Lound,
35 I know none so fair a maiden,
   As I go enslaved.
Sweet lady, I pray thee
   Love me a moment;
I will make known my song
40   To the one to whom it is due.

EXERCISES

1. The first lyric is written in the Southwestern dialect. Can you find a distinguishing dialect feature? (See p. 27.) What Southwestern features do you not find?
2. What verb form is *i-cumen* (3)? What are its two distinguishing features?
3. What is the regular third person singular present ending of the verb in the Southwestern dialect? Is it found here? How do you account for the ending of *springþ* (6) and *Lhouþ* (9)?
4. Comment on *Mę rewes* (2) in the second lyric and *mę reweþ* (14) in the third lyric.
5. The third lyric belongs to the Northeast Midland area. What Northern dialect feature do you find? What Northern features do you not find?
6. Does the ending of *lovest* (27) show the normal development of OE verbs? What were the *o* and *v* in this word in OE? Why did these letters change?
7. How is *Norhamptoun* spelled in MnE? How does the ME spelling reflect the word's etymology more clearly? How does *Averyl* (4) compare with the form in Chaucer's *General Prologue*, line 1? (For an explanation of the different forms, consult a dictionary for the etymology of *April*.)
8. What case does *mę* (13) reflect?
9. Explain the forms *nis* (13) and *nulle* (20).
10. Explain why the verb *tęne* (8) has as its ending neither *-es* nor *-eth*.
11. Is there any evidence of OE adverbial endings in the passage?

THE EARLY MODERN ENGLISH PERIOD[1]

William Caxton

From His Preface to Malory's *Le Morte Darthur*

TEXT

Thenne, al these thynges forsayd aledged, I
coude not wel denye but that there was suche a
noble kyng named Arthur, and reputed one of the
nine worthy, and fyrst and chyef of the Cristen
5 men. And many noble volumes be made of hym
and of his noble knyghtes in Frensshe, which
I have seen and redde beyonde the see, which
been not had in our maternal tongue. But in
Walsshe ben many, and also in Frensshe, and
10 somme in Englysshe, but nowher nygh alle.
Wherfore, suche as have late ben drawen oute
bryefly into Englysshe, I have, after the symple
connynge that God hath sente to me, under the
favour and correctyon of al noble lordes and
15 gentylmen, enprysed to enprynte a book of the
noble hystoryes of the sayd kynge Arthur and
of certeyn of his knyghtes, after a copye unto
me delyverd, whyche copye syr Thomas Malorye
dyd take oute of certeyn bookes of Frensshe
20 and reduced it into Englysshe.

And I, accordyng to my copye, have doon
sette it in enprynte to the entente that noble
men may see and lerne the noble actes of
chyvalrye, the jentyl and vertuous dedes that
25 somme knyghtes used in tho dayes, by whyche
they came to honour, and how they that were
vycious were punysshed and ofte put to shame
and rebuke; humbly bysechyng al noble lordes
and ladyes wyth al other estates, of what estate
30 or degree they been of, that shal see and rede
in this sayd book and werke, that they take the
good and honest actes in their remembraunce,
and to folowe the same; wherein they shalle
fynde many joyous and playsaunt hystoryes and
35 noble and renomed actes of humanyté, gentyl-
nesse, and chyvalryes. For herein may be seen
noble chyvalrye, curtosye, humanyté, frendly-
nesse, hardynesse, love, frendshyp, cowardyse,
murdre, hate, vertue, and synne. Doo after the
40 good and leve the evyl, and it shal brynge you
to good fame and renommee.

And for to passe the tyme thys book shal be
pleasunte to rede in, but for to gyve fayth and
byleve that al is trewe that is conteyned herin,
45 ye be at your lyberté. But al is wryton for our
doctryne, and for to beware that we falle not
to vyce ne synne, but t'exersyse and folowe
vertu, by whyche we may come and atteyne to
good fame and renommé in thys lyf, and after
50 thys shorte and transytorye lyf to come unto
everlastyng blysse in heven; the whyche He
graunte us that reygneth in heven, the Blessyd
Trynyté. AMEN.

Thenne, to procede forth in thys sayd book,
55 whyche I dyrecte unto alle noble prynces, lordes,
and ladyes, gentylmen or gentylwymmen, that
desyre to rede or here redde of the noble and
joyous hystorye of the grete conquerour and
excellent kyng, kyng Arthur, somtyme kyng of
60 thys noble royalme thenne callyd Bretaygne, I,
Wyllyam Caxton, symple persone, present thys
book folowyng whyche I have enprysed t'enprynte: and treateth of the noble actes, feates
of armes of chyvalrye, prowesse, hardynesse,
65 humanyté, love, curtosye, and veray gentyl-
nesse, wyth many wonderful hystoryes and
adventures.

[1] This period lasted from 1450–1700. Except for the Caxton
and Malory selections, which date from the late fifteenth century, the following texts belong to the late sixteenth and the
early seventeenth century.

Thomas Malory

From *Le Morte Darthur*

TEXT

Hit befel in the dayes of Uther Pendragon,
when he was kynge of all Englond and so regned,
that there was a myghty duke in Cornewaill that
helde warre ageynst hym long tyme, and the
5 duke was called the duke of Tyntagil. And so
by meanes kynge Uther send for this duk,
chargyng hym to brynge his wyf with hym,
for she was called a fair lady and a passynge
wyse, and her name was called Igrayne.
10 So whan the duke and his wyf were comyn
unto the kynge, by the meanes of grete lordes
they were accorded bothe: the kynge lyked and
loved this lady wel, and he made them grete
chere out of mesure and desyred to have lyen
15 by her. But she was a passyng good woman and
wold not assente unto the kynge.
And thenne she told the duke her husband
and said,
'I suppose that we were sente for that I shold
20 be dishonoured. Wherfor, husband, I counceille
yow that we departe from hens sodenly, that
we maye ryde all nyghte unto oure owne castell.'
And in lyke wyse as she saide so they departed,
that neyther the kynge nor none of his counceill
25 were ware of their departyng. Also soone as
kyng Uther knewe of theire departyng soo
sodenly, he was wonderly wrothe; thenne he
called to hym his pryvy counceille and told
them of the sodeyne departyng of the duke and
30 his wyf. Thenne they avysed the kynge to send
for the duke and his wyf by a grete charge:
'And yf he wille not come at your somons,
thenne may ye do your best; thenne have ye
cause to make myghty werre upon hym.'
35 Soo that was done, and the messagers hadde
their ansuers; and that was thys, shortly, that
neyther he nor his wyf wold not come at hym.
Thenne was the kyng wonderly wroth, and
thenne the kyng sente hym playne word ageyne
40 and badde hym be redy and stuffe hym and
garnysshe hym, for within forty dayes he wold

fetche hym oute of the byggest castell that he
hath. Whanne the duke hadde thys warnynge
anone he wente and furnysshed and garnysshed
45 two stronge castels of his, of the whiche the one
hyght Tyntagil and the other castel hyght
Terrabyl.
So his wyf dame Igrayne he putte in the
castell of Tyntagil, and hymself he putte in the
50 castel of Terrabyl, the whiche had many yssues
and posternes oute. Thenne in all haste came
Uther with a grete hoost and leyd a syege aboute
the castel of Terrabil, and ther he pyght many
pavelyons. And there was grete warre made on
55 bothe partyes and moche peple slayne.
Thenne for pure angre and for grete love of
fayr Igrayne the kyng Uther felle seke. So came
to the kynge Uther syre Ulfius, a noble knyght,
and asked the kynge why he was seke.
60 'I shall telle the,' said the kynge. 'I am seke
for angre and for love of fayre Igrayne, that I
may not be hool.'
'Wel, my lord,' said syre Ulfius, 'I shal seke
Merlyn and he shalle do yow remedy, that
65 youre herte shal be pleasyd.'

EXERCISES

1. These passages are examples of early EMnE with the original spelling. There had been no standard dialect in OE or ME, but largely because of the increasing importance of London as the commercial capital of England and because Caxton printed many books in the Southeast Midland dialect of London, the language of London became standard. There is also a tendency, with the printed word, toward standardization of spelling, although anything approaching complete standardization is still a very long way off. List Caxton's spellings that differ from present-day practice. How consistent is Caxton? What are the distinctive French spellings? (Caxton is usually credited with establishing the modern distinctions between *ee/ie* and *ea*, and between *oo* and *oa*. There is some evidence in these passages for the first distinction, but not enough for the second.)

2. Are there any deviations from present-day word order?

3. Do you find significant departures in word order from that of the ME selections? Do you find syntactical constructions that do not survive into standard MnE? How many of these have you noticed in OE or ME?

4. What archaic or obsolete words and word forms do you find?

5. Are there any inflectional endings that do not survive into present-day English?

6. How many French borrowings can you identify? To what aspect of life do many of the nouns pertain?

7. Is there still a distinction between the nominative and accusative forms of the second person personal pronoun? What distinctions are used to show familiarity and respect?

8. Find all the occurrences of *may* in the passages. With what sense is the word used? Is this the same sense as OE and ME usage? The same as present-day usage?

9. Find all the uses of *shall* and *will*. What meanings do they have? Compare with MnE usage.

10. In which instances have the meanings of prepositions changed since these selections were written?

11. Find an example of the survival of the OE passive verb with the meaning "is named."

12. Is the modern form *those* used in the passages? What form of the relative pronoun is preferred here? Which form is not used?

→ Commercial + gov't (judicial)

The Lord's Prayer

(Matthew 6: 9–13)

TEXT

Our father which art in heaüen,
hallowed be thy name.
Thy kingdome come. Thy will
be done, in earth, as it is in heauen.
5 Giue us this day our daily bread.
And forgiue us our debts, as we
forgiue our debters.
And lead us not into temptation,
but deliuer us from euill: For thine is
10 the kingdome, and the power, and the
glory, for euer, Amen.

TRANSCRIPTION

[əʊr feɪðə˞ hwɪč ɑɪrt ɪn hɛvn̩
hæləwɪd biː ðəɪ nɛɪm
ðəɪ kɪŋdəm kʊm ðəɪ wɪl
bɪ dʊn ɪn ɝθ əz ɪt ɪz ɪn hɛvn̩
5 gɪv ʊs ðɪs deɪ əʊr dɛɪlɨ brɛd
ænd fɔrgɪv ʊs əʊr dɛts əz wiː
fɔrgɪv əʊr dɛtə˞z
ænd leɪd ʊs nɔt ɪntʊ tɛmteɪsjən
bʊt dɪlɪvə˞ ʊs frəm iːvɪl fɔr ðəɪn ɪz
10 ðə kɪŋdəm ən ðə pəʊə˞ ən ðə
glɔɪrɨ fɔrɛvə˞ ɑmɛn]

EXERCISES

1. Compare this version of the prayer with the ME version and determine for yourself the sorts of differences and similarities that exist. Are the differences or the similarities more noticeable?

2. Do present-day spelling practices seem fairly well established here?

3. Make careful note of the features of the EMnE version of the prayer that do not conform to present-day practice. Now make your own translation into standard idiomatic present-day English and compare it with one of the recent standard translations.

The Prodigal Son

(*Luke* 15: 11–32)

TEXT	TRANSCRIPTION

<table>
<tr><td>

And hee ſaid, A certaine man had two ſonnes:
And the yonger of them ſaid to his father,
Father, giue me the portion of goods that <u>falleth</u>
to me. And he diuided unto them his liuing.

5   And not many dayes after, the yonger ſonne
gathered altogether, and tooke his iourney into
a farre countrey, and there waſted his ſubſtance
with riotous liuing. And when he had ſpent all,
there aroſe a mighty famine in that land, and he
10 beganne to be in want. And he went and ioyned
himſelfe to a citizen of that countrey, and he
ſent him into his fields to feed ſwine. And he
would faine haue filled his belly with the huſkes
that the ſwine did eate: ᵹ no man gaue unto him.

15   And when he came to himſelfe, he ſaid, How
many hired ſeruants of my fathers haue bread
inough and to ſpare, and I periſh with hunger ⁊
I will ariſe and goe to my father, and will ſay
unto him, Father, I haue ſinned againſt heauen
20 and before thee. And am no more worthy to be
called thy ſonne: make me as one of thy hired
ſeruants.

    And he aroſe and came to his father. But when
he was yet a great way off, his father ſaw him,
25 and had compaſſion, and ranne, and fell on his
necke, and kiſſed him. And the ſonne ſaid unto
him, Father, I haue ſinned againſt heauen, and
in thy ſight, and am no more worthy to be called
thy ſonne.

30   But the father ſaide to his ſeruants, Bring
foorth the beſt robe, and put it on him, and put
a ring on his hand, and ſhooes on his feete. And
bring hither the fatted calfe, and kill it, and let
us eate and be merrie. For this my ſonne was
35 dead, and is aliue againe; hee was loſt, ᵹ is
found. And they began to be merie.

    Now his elder ſonne was in the field, and as
he came and drew nigh to the houſe, he heard
muſicke ᵹ dauncing, And he called one of the
40 ſeruants, and aſked what theſe things meant.
And he ſaid unto him, Thy brother is come, and

</td><td>

[ænd iː sɛd ə saɪrtn̩ mæn æd tuː sʊnz ænd ðə
jʊŋgɚ əv ðəm sɛd tʊ ɪz fɛɪðɚ fɛɪðɚ gɪv miː ðə
pɔɪrsjən əv gʊɪdz ðət falɪθ tʊ miː ænd iː
dɪvəɪdɪd ʊntʊ ðəm ɪz lɪvɪn

ænd nɔt mɛnɪ dɛɪz æftɚ ðə jʊŋgɚ sʊn gɛɪðɚd   5
ɔɪltʊgɪðɚ ən tʊk ɪz ǰʊ̆nɪ ɪntʊ ə far kʊntrɪ ən
ðɛɪr wɜɪstɪd ɪz sʊbstənts wɪð rəɪətəs lɪvɪn ænd
hwɛn iː əd spɛnt ɔɪl ðɛɪr ərɔɪz ə məɪtɪ fæmɪn ɪn
ðæt lænd ən iː bɪgæn tʊ biː ɪn wɑnt ænd iː
wɛnt ən jɔɪnd ɪmsɛlf tʊ ə sɪtɪzən əv ðæt kʊntrɪ   10
ən iː sɛnt ɪm ɪntʊ ɪz fɪɪldz tʊ fɪɪd swəɪn ænd iː
wʊd fɛɪn əv fɪld ɪz bɛɫ wɪð ðə hʊsks ðət ðə
swəɪn dɪd ɛɪt ænd nɔɪ mæn gɛɪv ʊntʊ ɪm

ænd hwɛn iː kɛɪm tʊ ɪmsɛlf iː sɛd həʊ mɛnɪ
hɑɪrd saɪrvənts əv mɪ fɛɪðɚz əv brɛd ɪnʊf ən   15
tʊ spɛɪr ən əɪ pɛrɪš wɪθ hʊŋgɚ əɪ wɪl ərəɪz ən
gɔɪ tʊ mɪ fɛɪðɚ ən wɪl sɛɪ ʊntʊ ɪm fɛɪðɚ əɪ əv
sɪnd əgɛɪnst hɛvn̩ ən bɪfɔɪr ðiː ænd æm nɔɪ
mɔɪr wɜ̆ðɪ tʊ biː kɔld ðəɪ sʊn mɛɪk miː æz
ɔɪn əv ðəɪ hɑɪrd saɪrvənts   20

ænd iː ərɔɪz ən kɛɪm tʊ ɪz fɛɪðɚ bʊt hwɛn iː
wəz jɪt ə grɛɪt wɛɪ ɔɪf ɪz fɛɪðɚ sɔɪ ɪm ənæd
kəmpæsjən ən ræn ən fɛl ɔn ɪz nɛk ən kɪst ɪm
ænd ðə sʊn sɛd ʊntʊ ɪm fɛɪðɚ əɪ æv sɪnd
əgɛɪnst hɛvn̩ ən ɪn ðəɪ səɪt ən æm nɔɪ mɔɪr   25
wɜ̆ðɪ tʊ biː kɔld ðəɪ sʊn

bʊt ðə fɛɪðɚ sɛd tʊ ɪz saɪrvənts brɪŋ fɔɪrθ
ðə bɛst rɔɪb ən pʊt ɪt ɔn ɪm ən pʊt ə rɪŋ ɔn ɪz
hænd ən šuːz ɔn ɪz fɪɪt ænd brɪŋ hɪðɚ ðə fætɪd
kæf ən kɪl ɪt ən lɛt ʊs ɛɪt ən biː mɛrɪ fɔr ðɪs   30
məɪ sʊn wəz dɛd ən ɪz əlɛɪv əgɛn hiː wəz lɔst
ən ɪs fəʊnd ænd ðɛɪ bɪgɛn tʊ biː mɛrɪ

nəʊ ɪz ɛldɚ sʊn wəz ɪn ðə fɪɪld ən æz iː kɛɪm
ən druː nəɪ tʊ ðə həʊs iː hɜ̆d mjuːsɪk ən dænsɪn
ən iː kɔld ɔɪn əv ðə saɪrvənts ən æskt hwɛt   35
ðiːz θɪŋz mɛnt ænd iː sɛd ʊntʊ ɪm ðəɪ brʊðɚ
ɪz kʊm ən ðəɪ fɛɪðɚ æθ kɪld ðə fætɪd kæf
bɪkɔz iː æθ rɪsiːvd ɪm sɛlf ən səʊnd ænd iː wəz
æŋgrɪ ən wʊd nɔt gɔɪ ɪn ðɛɪrfɔɪr kɛɪm ɪz fɛɪðɚ
əʊt ən ɪntrɛɪtɪd ɪm   40

ænd iː ænsɚɪn sɛd tʊ ɪz fɛɪðɚ lɔɪ ðiːz mɛnɪ

</td></tr>
</table>

TEXT CONTINUED

thy father hath killed the fatted calfe, becauſe he hath receiued him ſafe and ſound. And he was angry, and would not goe in: therefore came
45 his father out, and intreated him.

And he anſwering ſaid to his father, Loe, theſe many yeeres doe I ſerue thee, neither tranſgreſſed I at any time thy commandement, and yet thou neuer gaueſt mee a kid, that I
50 might make merry with my friends: But as ſoone as this thy ſonne was come, which hath deuoured thy liuing with harlots, thou haſt killed for him the fatted calfe. And he ſaid unto him, Sonne, thou art euer with me, and all
55 that I haue is thine. It was meete that we ſhould make merry, and be glad: for this thy brother was dead, and is aliue againe: and was loſt, and is found.

TRANSCRIPTION CONTINUED

jɪrz duː əɪ sɑɪrv ðiː nɛɪðɚ trænsgrɛst əɪ æt ɛnɪ
təɪm ðəɪ kəmændmənt ən jɪt ðəu nɛvɚ gɛɪvɪst
miː ə kɪd ðət əɪ məɪt məɪk mɛrɪ wɪð məɪ frɛndz
bʊt əz suːn əz ðɪs ðəɪ sʊn wəz kʊm hwɪč æθ 45
dɪvəurd ðəɪ lɪvɪn wɪθ hɑrləts ðəu æst kɪld fɔr
ɪm ðə fætɪd kæɪf ænd iː sɛd ʊntʊ ɪm sʊn ðəu
ɑɪrt ɛvɚ wɪð miː ən ɔːl ðət əɪ hæv ɪz ðəɪn ɪt
wəz miːt ðət wiː šʊd məɪk mɛrɪ ən biː glæd
fɔr ðɪs ðəɪ brʊðɚ wəz dɛd ən ɪz ələɪv əgɛɪn 50
ən wəz lɔst ən ɪz fəund]

EXERCISES

1. Compare the EMnE long vowels in this selection with those of the corresponding ME long vowels in the ME *Prodigal Son*. Make careful note of the individual changes, and review the section on the Great Vowel Shift (pp. 29 ff.).

2. In comparison with present-day English, what are the most distinctive vowel sounds of EMnE? What is the vowel sound of *name, day, clean, great*? How are words pronounced in EMnE that are pronounced with [ʌ] in present-day English? (The quality of this EMnE sound, however, is debatable and may be [ʌ] as in present-day English.) Find examples in the selection.

3. What pronunciation does the spelling *–tion* or *–sion* signify? What is the sound of *er* in words like *verse, eternal*? (Note: this sound does not rhyme with the *ir* and *ur* of *bird* and *burn*.) What is the sound of *–ure*, as in *nature*? (The word is transcribed in Shakespeare's "Sonnet 18," below.) How does the pronunciation represented by the letters *–ing* differ from that of present-day English?

4. How many diphthongs does EMnE have in comparison to ME?

5. Refer to the vowel chart (p. 33) and determine the extent to which ME short vowels change when they

develop into EMnE. Find examples in the passage.

6. Study the EMnE practices of spelling, punctuation, and capitalization exemplified in this and succeeding passages. When is the long *s* (= ſ) not used? Does the letter *j* occur? the letter *v*? How are the quotations indicated? Is the use of capitalization consistent? What does the colon signify? Can you determine the general sort of reasoning behind EMnE punctuation practices? How consistent are spelling practices?

7. Are final *–e*'s pronounced? Are *–e–*'s in final unstressed syllables pronounced? What is the rhythmic effect in comparison to ME prose?

8. Carefully compare the word order of this passage with that of the ME *Prodigal Son*. Are the differences or the similarities more striking?

9. Are there any significant changes in syntactical constructions? (Do not overlook the double possessive in line 16. Compare it with the analogous construction in the ME selection.) Which relative pronoun is usurping part of the function of the more usual ME relative?

10. What is the ending of the third person singular present verb? Does this differ from the ME ending?

11. Compare the two passages for word choice. Which words are not used in the present passage? Which words replace them?

Francis Bacon
From "Of Discourse"

TEXT

SOme in their diſcourſe deſire rather commenda-
tion of wit in being able to holde all arguments,
then of iudgement in diſcerning what is true,
as if it were a praiſe to know what might be
5 ſaid, and not what ſhoulde bee thought. Some
haue certaine Common places and Theames
wherein they are good, and want varietie, which
kinde of pouertie is for the moſt part tedious,
and nowe and then ridiculous. The honourableſt
10 part of talke, is to guide the occaſion, and againe
to moderate & paſſe to ſomewhat elſe. It is good
to varie and mixe ſpeech of the preſent occaſion
with argument, tales with reaſons, asking of
queſtions, with telling of opinions, and ieſt with
15 earneſt. But ſome thinges are priuiledged from
ieſt, namely Religion, matters of ſtate, great
perſons, any mans preſent buſineſſe of importance, and any caſe that deſerueth pittie.
He that queſtioneth much ſhall learne much,
20 and content much, ſpecially if hee applie his
queſtions to the skill of the perſon of whom he
asketh, for he ſhal giue them occaſion to pleaſe
themſelues in ſpeaking, and himſelfe ſhall con-
tinually gather knowledge. If you diſſemble
25 ſometimes your knowledge of that you are
thought to knowe, you ſhall bee thought another
time to know that you know not. Speech of a
mans ſelfe is not good often, and there is but one
caſe, wherin a man may commend himſelfe
30 with good grace, and that is in commending
vertue in another, eſpecially if it be ſuch a
vertue, as whereunto himſelfe pretendeth. Diſcretion of ſpeech is more then eloquence, and
to ſpeake agreably to him, with whome we deale
35 is more then to ſpeake in good wordes or in good
order. A good continued ſpeech without a good
ſpeech of interlocution ſheweth ſlowneſſe: and
a good reply or ſecond ſpeech, without a good
ſet ſpeech ſheweth ſhallowneſſe and weaknes, as
40 wee ſee in beaſtes that thoſe that are weakeſt in
the courſe are yet nimbleſt in the turne. To

98

TRANSCRIPTION

[sʊm ɪn ðɛɪr dɪskoɪrs dɪsəɪr ræðɚ kəmendɛɪsjən
əv wɪt ɪn biɪn ɛɪbəl tʊ hoɪld ɔɪl ɑrgɪments
ðən əv jʊdjment ɪn dɪsɑɪrnɪn hwət ɪz truɪ əz ɪf
ɪt wɚ ə prɛɪz tʊ noɪ hwət məɪt bɪ sɛɪd ən nɑt
hwət šʊd bɪ ðɔɪt sʊm æv sɑɪrtɪn kʊmən plɛɪsɪz   5
ən tɛɪmz hwɛrɪn ðɛɪ ɚ gʊɪd ən wɑnt vərəɪətɪ
hwɪč kəɪnd əv pɑvɚtɪ ɪs fɔr ðə moɪst pɑɪrt
tiɪdjəs ən nəʊ ən ðɛn rɪdɪkɪləs ðə ɔnɚblɪst pɑɪrt
əv tɔɪk ɪz tʊ gəɪd ðəkɛɪzjən ən əgɛn tʊ mɑdɚɛɪt
ən pæs tʊ sʊmhwət ɛls ɪt ɪz gʊɪd tʊ vɛɪrɪ ən mɪks   10
spiɪč əv ðə prɛzənt əkɛɪzjən wɪð ɑrgɪment tɛɪlz
wɪð rɛɪzənz æskɪn əv kwɛɪstjənz wɪð tɛlɪn əv
əpɪnjənz ən jɛst wɪð ɚnɪst bʊt sʊm θɪŋgz ɚ
prɪvlɛjd frəm jɛst nɛɪmlɪ rɪlɪjən mætɚz əv stɛɪt
grɛɪt pɑɪrsənz ɛnɪ mænz prɛzənt bɪznɪs əv   15
ɪmpɔɪrtənts ən ɛnɪ kɛɪs ðət dɪzɑɪrvɪθ pɪtɪ hiɪ
ðət kwɛstjənɪθ mʊč šæl lɚn mʊč ən kəntent
mʊč spɛɪsjəlɪ ɪf iɪ əplɛɪ ɪz kwɛstjənz tʊ ðə skɪl
əv ðə pɑɪrsən əv huɪm iɪ æskɪθ fɔr iɪ šæl gɪv
ðəm əkɛɪzjən tʊ plɛɪz ðɛmsɛlvz ɪn spɛɪkɪn ən   20
ɪmsɛlf šæl kəntɪnjəlɪ gɛɪðɚ noɪləj ɪf juɪ dɪsɛmbəl
sʊmtɛɪmz jɚ noɪləj əv ðæt juɪ ɚ θɪɪt tʊ noɪ juɪ
šæl bɪ θɔɪt ənoɪðɚ tɛɪm tʊ noɪ ðət juɪ noɪ nɑt
spiɪč əv ə mænsɛlf ɪz nɑt gʊɪd ɔɪfn ən ðɛɪr ɪs
bʊt oɪn kɛɪs hwɛrɪn ə mæn mɛɪ kəmend ɪmsɛlf   25
wɪθ gʊɪd grɛɪs ən ðæt ɪz ɪn kəmɛndɪn vɑɪrtə
ɪn ənʊðɚ espɛɪsjəlɪ ɪf ɪt biɪ sʊč ə vɑɪrtə əz
hwɛrəntʊ ɪmsɛlf prɪtɛndɪθ dɪskrɛɪsjən əv spiɪč
ɪz moɪr ðən ɛləkwɪnts ən tʊ spɛɪk əgriɪəblɪ tʊ
hɪm wɪðhuɪm wiɪ dɛɪl ɪz moɪr ðən tʊ spɛɪk ɪn   30
gʊɪd wɚdz ɚ ɪn gʊɪd oɪrdɚ ə gʊɪd kəntɪnjəd
spiɪč wɪðəʊt ə gʊɪd spiɪč əv ɪntɚloɪkjuɪsjən
šoɪwɪθ sloɪnɪs ən ə gʊɪd rɪplɛɪ ɚ sɛɪkən spiɪč
wɪðəʊt ə gʊɪd sɛt spiɪč šoɪwɪθ šælənɪs ən wɛɪknɪs
əz wiɪ siɪ ɪn bɛɪsts ðət ðoɪz ðət ɚ wɛɪkɪst ɪn ðə   35
koɪrs ɑr jɪt nɪmblɪst ɪn ðə tɚn tʊ juɪz tuɪ mɛn
sɚkəmstæntsɪz ɛɪr oɪn kʊm tʊ ðə mætɚ ɪz
wɛɪrɪsəm tʊ juɪz noɪn ət ɔɪl ɪz blʊnt]

Richard Hooker

From A Sermon on St. Jude's Epistle

TEXT

HAving otherwhere ſpoken of the words of *Saint
Iude*, going next before, concerning *Mockers*,
which ſhould come in the laſt time, & back-
ſliders, which even then fell away from the faith
5 of our Lord and Saviour Ieſus Chriſt; I am now
by the aide of almighty God, and through the
aſſiſtance of his good ſpirit, to lay before you
the words of exhortation, which I haue read.

2 Wherein firſt of all, whoſoever hath an eie
10 to ſee, let him open it, and he ſhall wel perceiue,
how carefull the Lord is for his children, how
deſirous to ſee them profit and growe vp to a
manly ſtature in Chriſt, how loath to haue them
any way miſlead, either by examples of the
15 wicked, or by enticements of the world, and by
provocation of the fleſh, or by any other meanes
forcible to deceaue them, and likely to eſtrange
their heart from God. For God is not at that
point with vs, that hee careth not whether wee
20 ſinke or ſwimme. No, he hath written our names
in the palme of his hand, in the ſignet vpon his
finger are we graven, in ſentences not onely of
mercy, but of iudgement alſo we are remembred.
He never denoūceth iudgements againſt the
25 wicked, but hee maketh ſome *Proviſo* for his
children, as it were for ſome certaine priviledged
perſons, *Touch not mine annointed, doe my
Prophets no harme, hurt not the earth, nor the
ſea, nor the trees, till wee haue ſealed the ſervants
30 of God in their foreheads.* Hee never ſpeaketh of
godleſſe men, but he adioineth words of comfort,
or admonition, or exhortation, whereby wee are
moued to reſt and ſettle our hearts on him.

TRANSCRIPTION

[hævɪn ʊðɚhwɛr spoːkən əv ðə wɝdz əv sɛɪnt
juːd goːɪn nɛkst bɪfoːr kənsɑːrnɪn mɔkɚz hwɪč
šʊd kʊm ɪn ðə læst təɪm ən bæksləɪdɚz hwɪč
iːvən ðɛn fɛl əwɛː frəm ðə fɛɪθ əv ɚ lɔrd ən
sɛɪvjɚ jiːzəs krəɪst əɪ əm nəʊ bəɪ ðə ɛɪd əv   5
ɔːlməɪtɪ gɔd ən ðruː ðə əsɪstənts əv ɪz gʊːd
spɪrɪt tʊ lɛː bɪfoːr juː ðə wɝdz əv ɛksɚtɛɪsjən
hwɪč əɪ əv rɪd

hwɛrɪn fɝst əv ɔːl huːsoːɛvɚ æθ ən əɪ tʊ siː
lɛt ɪm oːpən ɪt ən iː šæl wɛl pɚsɛɪv həʊ kærfəl   10
ðə lɔrd ɪs fɚ ɪz čɪldrən həʊ dɪsəɪrəs tʊ siː ðəm
proːfɪt ən groː ʊp tʊ ə mænlɪ stætɚ ɪn krəɪst
əʊ loːθ tʊ æv ðəm ɛnɪ wɛː mɪslɛd ɛɪðɚ bəɪ
ɛgzæmpəlz əv ðə wɪkɪd ɚ bəɪ ɪntəɪsmənts əv
ðə wɝld ən bəɪ provəkɛɪsjən əv ðə flɛš ɚ bəɪ   15
ɛnɪ ʊðɚ mɛɪnz foːrsɪbəl tʊ dɪsɛɪv ðəm ən ləɪklɪ
tʊ əstrɛɪnj ðɛɪr hɑːrt frəm gɔd fɚ gɔd ɪs nɔt
ət ðæt pəɪnt wɪð ʊs ðət iː kɛɪrɪθ nɔt hwɛðɚ wiː
sɪŋk ɚ swɪm noː iː əθ wrɪtn̩ əʊr nɛɪmz ɪn ðə
pɑːm əv ɪz hænd ɪn ðə sɪgnət ʊpon ɪz fɪŋgɚ ɑr   20
wiː grɛɪvən ɪn sɛntənsɪz nɔt oːnlɪ əv mɝsɪ bʊt
əv jʊdjmənt ɔːlsoː wiː ɚ rɪmɛmbrɪd hiː nɛvɚ
dɪnəʊnsɪθ jʊdjmənts əgɛɪnst ðə wɪkɪd bʊt iː
mɛɪkɪθ sʊm prəvəɪzoː fɚ ɪz čɪldrən əz ɪt wɝ
fɚ sʊm sɑːrtɪn prɪvlɪjd pɑːrsənz tʊč nɔt məɪn   25
ənəɪntɪd duː məɪ proːfɪts noː hɑːrm hɝt nɔt ðə
ɝθ nɔːr ðə siː nɔːr ðə triːz tɪl wiː əv sɛɪld ðə
sɑːrvənts əv gɔd ɪn ðɛɪr foːrɛdz hiː nɛvɚ spɛɪkɪθ
əv gɔdləs mɛn bʊt iː əjəɪnɪθ wɝdz əv kʊmfɚt
ɚ ædmənɪsjən ɚ ɛksɚtɛɪsjən hwɛrbəɪ wiː ɚ   30
mʊvd tʊ rɛst ən sɛtəl əʊr hɑːrts ɔn ɪm]

BACON TEXT CONTINUED

vſe too many circumſtances ere one come to
the matter is weariſome, to vſe none at all is
blunt.

EXERCISES

1. As a way of perceiving the rich possibilities of EMnE prose, do a comparative stylistic analysis of these selections, paying attention to general patterns of word order and syntax and to the various types of clauses; note too the rhetorical treatment of rhythm, balance, and the like.

2. As a way of studying the development of English prose, perhaps you might try to compare these selections with the original OE prose of *Alfred's Prayer* and *The Anglo-Saxon Chronicle*, and with the ME passages from *The Parson's Tale* and *A Treatise on the Astrolabe*—and maybe with Caxton's and Malory's fifteenth-century prose. Note, especially, general sentence patterns, word order, the presence and use of function words and connectives, and the ways sentences, clauses, and phrases begin. Offer evidence for each generalization you make, realizing that such generalizations should only be tentative, since your evidence is limited.

3. Although the meanings are apparent, are the following key words precisely the ones that would be used in present-day English? Bacon: *somewhat* (11), *that* (25, 27), *wherin* (29), *as whereunto* (32); Hooker: *otherwhere* (1), *wherin* (9), *whosoever* (9), *but* (25, 31).

4. What other words in these passages do not sound quite right to us? How would you translate them into present-day English? Beyond the matters already considered, if these selections were read aloud today with standard English pronunciation, would a general audience have any particular feeling about the language used? Explain.

5. Has the modern form *those* developed by Bacon's time? What are the ME and OE forms?

6. Is Bacon's pronunciation of *one* the present-day pronunciation? What is the etymological relation of *one* to *only* (Hooker, 22)? What is the precise phonological difference today?

7. How does Bacon indicate the possessive case?   *many*

8. How does Bacon spell *then* and *than*? Are these words etymological doublets?

William Shakespeare

(Hamlet III, ii, 1–29, First Folio)

TEXT

Ham. Speake the Speech I pray you, as I
pronounc'd it to you trippingly on the Tongue:
But if you mouth it, as many of your Players
do, I had as liue the Town-Cryer had ſpoke my
5 Lines: Nor do not ſaw the Ayre too much [with?]
your hand thus, but vſe all gently; for in the
verie Torrent, Tempeſt, and (as I may ſay) the
Whirle-winde of Paſſion, you muſt acquire and
beget a Temperance that may giue it Smooth-
10 neſſe. O it offends mee to the Soule, to ſee a
robuſtious Pery-wig-pated Fellow, teare a Paſſion to tatters, to verie ragges, to ſplit the eares
of the Groundlings: who (for the moſt part)
are capeable of nothing, but inexplicable
15 dumbe ſhewes, & noiſe: I could haue ſuch a
Fellow whipt for o're-doing Termagant: it out-
Herod's Herod. Pray you auoid it.
　Player. I warrant your Honor.
　Ham. Be not too tame neyther: but let your
20 owne Diſcretion be your Tutor. Sute the Action
to the Word, the Word to the Action, with this
ſpeciall obſeruance: That you ore-ſtop [=ore-
ſtep?] not the modeſtie of Nature; for any thing
ſo ouer-done, is frō the purpoſe of Playing,
25 whoſe end both at the firſt and now, was and is,
to hold as 'twer the Mirrour vp to Nature; to
ſhew Vertue her owne Feature, Scorne her owne
Image, and the verie Age and Bodie of the Time,
his forme and preſſure. Now, this ouer-done, or
30 come tardie off, though it make the vnskilfull
laugh, cannot but make the Iudicious greeue [.]

TRANSCRIPTION

Ham. [spɛːk ðə spiːč əɪ prɛː juː əz əɪ prənəunst
ɪt tʊ juː trɪpn̩lɪ ɔn ðə tʊŋ bət ɪf juː məʊð ɪt
əz mɛnɪ əv jɚ plɛɪɚz duː əɪd əz liːv ðə təʊn
krəɪɚ əd spoːk mɪ ləɪnz nɔːr dʊ nɔt sɔː ðə ɛːr
tuː mʊč (wɪð) jɚ hænd ðʊs bət juːz ɔːl ǰentlɪ 5
fɚ ɪn ðə vɛːrɪ tɔrənt tɛmpɪst ænd əz əɪ mɛː sɛː
ðə hwɝ̩lwɪnd əv pæsjən juː mʊst əkwəɪɚ ən
bɪgɪt ə tɛmprənts ðət mɛː gɪv ɪt smuːðnɪs oː
ɪt əfɛnz mɪ tʊ ðə soːl tʊ siː ə rəbʊstjəs pɛrɪwɪg
pɛːtɪd fɛloː tɛːr ə pæsjən tʊ tætɚz tʊ vɛrɪ 10
rægz tʊ splɪt ðə ɛːrz əv ðə grəʊnlɪnz hʊ fɚ ðə
moːst pɑːrt ɚ kɛːpəbl̩ əv nɔːθŋ bət ɪnɛksplɪkəbl̩
dʊm šoːz ən nəɪz əɪ kʊd əv sʊč ə fɛloː hwɪpt
fɚ oːrduːɪn tɑːrməgənt ɪt əʊt hɛrədz hɛrəd prɛː
juː əvəɪd ɪt 15
　Player. əɪ wɑrənt jɚ ɔnɚ
　Ham. biː nɔt tuː tɛːm nɛːðɚ bət lɛt jɚ oːn
dɪskrɛsjən bɪ jɚ tjuːtɚ sjuːt ðə æksjən tʊ ðə
wɝ̩d ðə wɝ̩d tʊ ðə æksjən wɪð ðɪs spɛsjəl
əbzɑːrvənts ðət juː oːrstɛp nɔt ðə mɑdəstɪ əv 20
nɛɪtɚ fɚ ɛnɪ θɪŋ soː oːvɚdʊn ɪz frɑm ðə pɝ̩pəs
əv plɛɪɪn huːz end boːθ ət ðə fɝ̩st ən nəʊ wəz
ənd ɪz tʊ hoːld əstwɚ ðə mɪrɚ ʊp tʊ nɛɪtɚ tʊ
šoː vɑːrtə hɚ oːn fɛɪtɚ skɔːrn ɚ oːn ɪmɪǰ ən ðə
vɛrɪ ɛɪǰ ən bɔdɪ əv ðə təɪm ɪz fɔːrm ən prɛsɚ 25
nəʊ ðɪs oːvɚdʊn ɚ kʊm tɑːrdɪ ɔːf ðoː ɪt mɛːk
ðə ʊnskɪlfʊl læf kænɔt bət mɛːk ðə ǰʊdɪsjəs
griːv]

EXERCISES

1. Is there any distinction in the sounds represented by the letters *ee/ie* and *ea* in EMnE? (See the first and last lines.) Compare present-day English practice.

2. How many nouns and adjectives here are Latin borrowings? (Consult as well the two selections following.) Why is it often difficult in EMnE to tell whether a given word is borrowed from French or from Latin?

3. Assuming present-day stress patterns, and using marks representing only stressed and unstressed syllables, mark these Latinate borrowings for stress. Now comparing this passage with a passage of OE prose, can you suggest how the massive influx of Latinate words in the ME and Renaissance periods affected the rhythmic "flow" of English prose? Examine Shakespeare's sonnets below and comment on the metrical effect of this influx. Examine a passage of Chaucer's verse above to the same end. (In Chaucer's language the percentage of French borrowings in relation to the percentage of direct Latin borrowings is greater than it is in Shakespeare's language, since the period of greatest Latin borrowings is the Renaissance.)

4. What specific Latinate prefixes occur in EMnE? Do some of these appear in ME as well? Do any occur in OE?

5. Compounding has been an active principle of word formation in all periods of English. Find examples in this selection.

6. Can you find any expressions, word forms, or syntactical patterns that have not normally developed into present-day standard colloquial English? Are there very many?

7. With what form of the second person personal pronoun does Hamlet address the Player? Is this the polite or the familiar/contemptuous form? Does Shakespeare make use of the distinction in his plays? (Read carefully *Othello* I, i,) Cf. *Sonnet 18*, below.

8. Shakespeare was one of those who introduced into the language new words based on Latinate forms. Many of these words remain in the language, so that when we see them in his plays we do not recognize them as lexical innovations. Some others, however, do not remain, and these, therefore, are fairly easy to find. For a major project, read an entire Shakespearean play and make a study of Shakespeare's "inkhorn" terms which do not remain in the language.

William Shakespeare

Sonnet 116

<table>
<tr><td>

TEXT

LEt me not to the marriage of true mindes
Admit impediments, loue is not loue
Which alters when it alteration findes,
Or bends with the remouer to remoue.
5 O no, it is an euer fixed marke
That lookes on tempeſts and is neuer ſhaken;
It is the ſtar to euery wandring barke,
Whoſe worths vnknowne, although his higth be
    taken.
Lou's not Times foole, though roſie lips and
    cheeks
10 Within his bending ſickles compaſſe come,
Loue alters not with his breefe houres and
    weekes,
But beares it out euen to the edge of doome:
  If this be error and vpon me proued,
  I neuer writ, nor no man euer loued.

</td><td>

TRANSCRIPTION

[lɛt miː nɔt tʊ ðə mærɪǰ əv truː məɪndz
ədmɪt ɪmpɛdɪmənts lʊv ɪz nɔt lʊv
hwɪč ɔːltɚz hwɛn ɪt ɔːltərɛːsjən fəɪndz
ɔr bɛndz wɪð ðə rɪmuːvɚ tʊ rɪmuːv
ɔː noː ɪt ɪz ən ɛvɚ fɪksɪd mɑːrk   5
ðət lʊks ɔn tɛmpɪsts ənd ɪz nɛvɚ šɛːkn̩
ɪt ɪs ðə stɑːr tʊ ɛvrɪ wɑndrɪn bɑːrk
huːz wɚθs ʊnːoːn ɔːlðoː ɪz həɪθ bɪ tɛːkn̩
lʊvz nɔt təɪmz fuːl ðoː roːzɪ lɪps ən čiːks
wɪðɪn ɪz bɛndn̩ sɪkl̩z kʊmpəs kʊm   10
lʊv ɔːltɚz nɔt wɪð ɪz briːf oːrz ən wiːks
bət bɛːrz ɪt əʊt iːn tʊ ðɪ ɛǰ əv duːm
ɪf ðɪs biː ɛrɚ ənd əpɔn miː pruːvd
əɪ nɛvɚ rɪt nɔːr noː mæn ɛvɚ lʊvd]

</td></tr>
</table>

William Shakespeare

Sonnet 18

TEXT

SHall I compare thee to a Summers day?
Thou art more louely and more temperate:
Rough windes do ſhake the darling buds of
    Maie,
And Sommers leaſe hath all too ſhort a date:
5 Sometime too hot the eye of heauen ſhines,
And often is his gold complexion dimm'd,
And euery faire from faire ſome-time declines,
By chance, or natures changing courſe vntrim'd:
But thy eternall Sommer ſhall not fade,
10 Nor looſe poſſeſſion of that faire thou ow'ſt,
Nor ſhall death brag thou wandr'ſt in his ſhade,
When in eternall lines to time thou grow'ſt,
    So long as men can breath or eyes can ſee,
    So long liues this, and this giues life to thee,

TRANSCRIPTION

[šæl əi kəmpɛɪr ðiː tʊ ə sʊmɚz dɛɪ
ðəʊ ɑɪrt mɔɪr lʊvlɪ ənd mɔɪr tɛmpərɛɪt
rʊf wəɪndz duː šɛɪk ðə dɑɪrlɪn bʊdz əv mɛɪ
ənd sʊmɚz lɛɪs əθ ɔɪl tuː šɔɪrt ə dɛɪt
ənd sʊmtəɪm tuː hɔt ðɪ əi əv hɛvn̩ šəɪnz   5
ənd ɔɪfn̩ ɪz ɪz gɔɪld kəmplɛksjən dɪmd
ənd ɛvrɪ fɛɪr frəm fɛɪr sʊmtəɪm dɪkləɪnz
bɪ čænts ɚ nɛɪtɚz čɛɪnjn̩ kɔɪrs ʊntrɪmd
bət ðəɪ ɪtɑɪrnəl sʊmɚ šæl nɔt fɛɪd
nɔɪr luɪz pəzɛsjən əv ðæt fɛɪr ðəʊ ɔɪst   10
nɔɪr šæl dɛθ bræg ðəʊ wandɚst ɪn ɪz šɛɪd
hwɛn ɪn ɪtɑɪrnəl ləɪnz tʊ təɪm ðəʊ grɔɪst
sɔɪ lɔŋ əz mɛn kən brɛɪð ɚ əɪz kən siː
sɔɪ lɔŋ lɪvz ðɪs ənd ðɪs gɪvz ləɪf tʊ ðiː]

EXERCISES

1. What function does the apostrophe have in these sonnets? Is Shakespeare's use of it consistent? What bearing does this have on whether or not unstressed ĕ should be pronounced?

2. What do the unstressed ĕ's in final syllables signify in words like *mindes* (#116, 1), *lookes* (#116, 6), and *barke* (#116, 7)?

3. What evidence can you think of for the pronunciation given for *euen* (#116, 12)? How do you account for the pronunciation given for *his* (#116, 8)?

4. Is the letter *k* pronounced in *vnknowne* (#116, 8)? (The same is probably true for *g* in words that had initial *gn–* in ME. Cf. MnE [næt] and [nɔ].)

5. In #116, what consonant is transcribed as a long consonant? Can you think of similar examples in MnE? Do we normally speak of long consonants in MnE?

6. Notice the occurrence of *whoſe* (#116, 8). Consult the *OED* to see when it came into the language.

7. How does Shakespeare pronounce the word *higth* (#116, 8)? Does this pronunciation survive today? Is there an alternate pronunciation? What is the pronunciation of *gh* in *although* (#116, 8) and *though* (#116, 9)? (What is the relationship of these two words etymologically?) Cf. the *gh* sound of *rough* (#18, 3). Trace the etymology of the following words: *light, delight, daughter, enough, laugh, trough, slough*.

8. What is the pronunciation of the "rhyme" words *proued* (#116, 13), *loued* (#116, 14)? What conclusion can you draw about rhyme evidence used to establish EMnE pronunciation?

9. What is Shakespeare's pronunciation of *often* (#18, 6)? What is yours? Is there a modern alternative? How do you explain phonologically the suppression of the *t*? (Cf. *glisten, listen, soften*.)

10. In *Sonnet 18*, how does Shakespeare's use of *all* (4) and *sometime* (5) differ from ours?

SELECTED BIBLIOGRAPHY

Convenient phonetic transcriptions of older periods of the language may be found in Kökeritz, *A Guide to Chaucer's Pronunciation*; Kökeritz, *Shakespeare's Pronunciation*; Marckwardt, *Introduction to the English Language*; and Moore, *Historical Outlines of English Sounds and Inflections*.

Allen, Harold B., ed. *Linguistics and English Linguistics*. New York: Appleton-Century-Crofts (Goldentree Bibliographies), 1966.

Anderson, Marjorie, and Blanche C. Williams. *Old English Handbook*. Cambridge, Mass.: Houghton Mifflin, 1935.

Baugh, Albert C. *A History of the English Language*. 2nd ed. New York: Appleton-Century-Crofts, 1957.

Bender, Harold H. *The Home of the Indo-Europeans*. Princeton: Princeton University Press, 1922.

Bloomfield, Morton W., and Leonard Newmark. *A Linguistic Introduction to the History of English*. New York: Alfred A. Knopf, 1963.

Bryant, Margaret M., *Modern English and Its Heritage*, 2nd ed., New York: Macmillan, 1962.

Bülbring, Karl D. *Altenglisches Elementarbuch. I. Teil: Lautlehre*. Heidelberg: Carl Winter's Universitätsbuchhandlung, 1902.

Campbell, A. *Old English Grammar*. Oxford: Oxford University Press, 1959.

Clark, John W. *Early English*. London: Andre Deutsch, 1957.

Cragie, William A., and James R. Hulbert, eds. *A Dictionary of American English on Historical Principles*. 4 vols. Chicago: University of Chicago Press, 1938–1944.

Dobbie, Elliott V. K., "Pronunciation." In *The Reader's Encyclopedia of Shakespeare*, ed. Oscar J. Campbell and Edward G. Quinn. New York: Thomas Y. Crowell, 1966.

Dobson, E. J. *English Pronunciation, 1500–1700*. 2 vols. Oxford: Oxford University Press, 1957.

Emerson, Oliver F. *A Middle English Reader*. New and revised ed. New York: Macmillan, 1915. Reprinted 1960.

Francis, W. Nelson. *The Structure of American English* with a chapter on American English dialects by Raven I. McDavid, Jr. New York: Ronald Press, 1958.

Gelb, I. J. *A Study of Writing*. Revised ed. Chicago: University of Chicago Press, 1963.

Hall, John R. Clark. *A Concise Anglo-Saxon Dictionary*. 4th ed. with Supplement by Herbert D. Meritt. Cambridge: Cambridge University Press, 1960.

Hall, Robert A., Jr. *Linguistics and Your Language*. Garden City, New York: Doubleday & Co., 1960. (Originally pub. as *Leave Your Language Alone!* [Ithaca, N. Y.: Linguistica, 1950].)

Hughes, John P. *The Science of Language: An Introduction to Linguistics*. New York: Random House, 1962.

Jespersen, Otto. *Growth and Structure of the English Language*. 9th ed. Oxford: Basil Blackwell, 1962.

———. *A Modern English Grammar on Historical Principles*. 7 vols. Copenhagen: Einar Munksgaard, 1909–1949.

Jordan, Richard. *Handbuch der Mittelenglischen Grammatik. I. Teil: Lautlehre*. Heidelberg: Carl Winter's Universitätsbuchhandlung, 1925.

Kennedy, Arthur G. *Current English*. Boston: Ginn, 1935.

Kökeritz, Helge. *A Guide to Chaucer's Pronunciation*. New Haven: Whitlock, 1954.

———. *Shakespeare's Pronunciation*. New Haven: Yale University Press, 1953.

Krapp, George Philip. *Modern English, Its Growth and Present Use*. Revised ed. by Albert H. Marckwardt. New York: Charles Scribner's Sons, 1969. (Originally pub. in 1909.)

Kurath, Hans, and Sherman M. Kuhn, eds. *Middle English Dictionary*. Ann Arbor: University of Michigan Press, 1952—. In progress.

Laird, Charlton. *The Miracle of Language*. Greenwich, Conn.: Fawcett, 1963. (Originally pub. in 1953.)

——— and Robert M. Gorrell. *English As Language: Backgrounds, Development, Usage*. New York: Harcourt, Brace & World, 1961.

Lehmann, Winifred P. *Historical Linguistics: An Introduction*. New York: Holt, Rinehart and Winston, 1962.

Marckwardt, Albert H. *American English*. New York: Oxford University Press, 1958.

Marckwardt, Albert H. *Introduction to the English Language.* New York: Oxford University Press, 1942.

Markman, Alan M., and Erwin R. Steinberg. *English Then and Now: Readings and Exercises.* New York: Random House, 1970.

Mathews, Mitford M., ed. *A Dictionary of Americanisms on Historical Principles.* 2 vols. Chicago: University of Chicago Press, 1951. Third impression, 1956.

McKnight, George H. *Modern English in the Making.* New York: Appleton-Century-Crofts, 1928 (OP).

McLaughlin, John C. *Aspects of the History of English.* New York: Holt, Rinehart and Winston, 1970.

Mencken, H. L. *The American Language.* 4th ed. and two supplements abridged, with annotations and new material by Raven I. McDavid, Jr., with the assistance of David W. Maurer. New York: Alfred A. Knopf, 1963.

Moore, Samuel. *Historical Outlines of English Sounds and Inflections.* Revised by Albert H. Marckwardt. Ann Arbor: George Wahr, 1957.

—— and Thomas A. Knott. *The Elements of Old English.* Revised by James R. Hulbert. 10th ed. Ann Arbor: George Wahr, 1955.

Mossé, Fernand. *A Handbook of Middle English.* Translated by James A. Walker. Baltimore: Johns Hopkins Press, 1952.

Murray, J. A. H. et al., eds. *Oxford English Dictionary.* 12 vols. Oxford: Oxford University Press, 1884–1928. *Supplement,* 1933.

Mustanoja, Tauno F. *A Middle English Syntax, Part I: Parts of Speech.* Helsinki: Société néophilologique, 1960.

Partridge, Eric, ed. *A Dictionary of Slang and Unconventional English.* 5th ed. 2 vols. in 1. New York: Macmillan, 1961.

Peters, Robert A. *A Linguistic History of English.* Boston: Houghton Mifflin, 1968.

Potter, Simeon. *Our Language.* Revised ed. Baltimore: Penguin, 1966.

Pyles, Thomas. *The Origins and Development of the English Language.* New York: Harcourt, Brace & World, 1964.

——. *Words and Ways of American English.* New York: Random House, 1952.

Quirk, Randolph, and C. L. Wrenn. *An Old English Grammar.* New York: Holt, Rinehart & Winston, n.d.

Robertson, Stuart. *The Development of Modern English.* 2nd ed. Revised by Frederic G. Cassidy. Englewood Cliffs, N. J.: Prentice-Hall, 1954.

Schlauch, Margaret. *The English Language in Modern Times (since 1400).* Warsaw: PWN–Polish Scientific Publishers, 1959.

Scott, Charles T., and Jon L. Erickson. *Readings for the History of the English Language.* Boston: Allyn and Bacon, 1968.

Serjeantson, Mary S. *A History of Foreign Words in English.* London: Routledge and Kegan Paul, 1935. Second impression, 1961.

Sheard, J. A. *The Words of English.* New York: Norton, 1966. (Originally pub. as *The Words We Use,* 1954.)

Sievers, Eduard. *An Old English Grammar.* Translated and edited by Albert S. Cook. 3rd ed. Boston: Ginn, 1903.

Skeat, Walter W. *A Concise Etymological Dictionary of the English Language.* Oxford: Clarendon Press, 1911. (Originally pub. as *An Etymological Dictionary of the English Language,* 1882.)

Stevick, Robert D. *English and Its History: The Evolution of A Language.* Boston: Allyn and Bacon, 1968.

Thieme, Paul. "The Indo-European Language." *Scientific American* 149 (October, 1958): 63–74.

Wardale, E. E. *An Introduction to Middle English.* London: K. Paul, Trench, Trubner, 1937.

Webster's Third New International Dictionary of the English Language. Springfield, Mass.: G. & C. Merriam, 1961.

Wentworth, Harold, and Stuart B. Flexner, eds. *Dictionary of American Slang.* New York: Thomas Y. Crowell, 1960. Reissued with supplement by Stuart B. Flexner, 1967.

Wright, Joseph, and Elizabeth M. *An Elementary Middle English Grammar.* 2nd ed. London: Oxford University Press, 1928.

——. *Old English Grammar.* 3rd ed. Oxford: Oxford University Press, 1925. Reprinted 1954.

Wyld, Henry C. *A Short History of English.* 3rd ed. New York: John Murray, 1927. Reprinted 1963.

Zachrisson, R. E. *Pronunciation of English Vowels, 1400–1700.* Göteborg, Sweden, 1913.

SELECTED DISCOGRAPHY

Although there are other good records available, the following are especially recommended. The first four are considered to be among the very best, particularly Ayres and Kökeritz. In listening to these records and to the one attached to the present textbook, the student should note the various readers' diversity of pronunciation. All of the recordings (except Ayres) are accompanied by texts.

Ayres, Harry Morgan. [Selections from *Beowulf*, Chaucer, Shakespeare, and *The Gettysburg Address*.] The National Council of Teachers of English P4PM–4852, P4PM–4853. [Has commentaries on pronunciation. Includes the *Beowulf* and *Hamlet* selections in the present textbook.]

Bessinger, J. B., Jr. *Beowulf, Caedmon's Hymn and Other Old English Poems*. Caedmon TC1161. [Lively readings, accompanied by a reconstructed six-stringed harp. Includes the *Beowulf* and "Cædmon's Hymn" selections in the present textbook.]

Coghill, Nevill, Norman Davis, and John Burrow. *Chaucer: The Canterbury Tales. The Prologue*. Argo RG 401. [Spirited interpretations by eminent scholars. Includes the "General Prologue" selection in the present textbook.]

Kökeritz, Helge. *A Thousand Years of English Pronunciation*. Educational Audio Visual LE 7650/55. [Extensive readings in OE, ME, and EMnE.]

Other Old English Recordings

Pope, John, and Helge Kökeritz. *Beowulf and Chaucer*. Available on tape from Educational Audio-Visual, Inc., Pleasantville, N. Y. 10570. [Pope's readings of *Beowulf* demonstrate his theory of rhythm and metrics. Kökeritz reads portions of the following: "The General Prologue," "The Wife of Bath's Prologue," "The Prioress's Tale," and *Troilus and Criseyde*. The readings include portions of the *Beowulf*, of the "General Prologue," and of the *Troilus and Criseyde* selections in the present textbook.]

Raffel, Burton, and Robert P. Creed. *Lyrics from the Old English*. Folkways FL 9858. [Thirteen selections, including six riddles, read in OE and in MnE. Includes the "Cædmon's Hymn" selection in the present textbook.]

Other Middle English Recordings

Bessinger, J.B., Jr. *The Canterbury Tales, Chaucer*. Caedmon TC 1151. [Contains "The General Prologue," "Prologue to the Parson's Tale," and "Chaucer's Retraction." Includes the "General Prologue" selection in the present textbook.]

———. *Chaucer: Two Canterbury Tales, the Miller's Tale and Reeve's Tale*. Caedmon TC 1223.

Borroff, Marie, and J. B. Bessinger, Jr. *Dialogues from Sir Gawain and the Green Knight and Pearl*. Caedmon TC 1192.

Burrow, John, Nevill Coghill, Norman Davis, and Lena Davis. *Chaucer: The Nun's Priest's Tale*. Argo RG 466. [Contains other Chaucerian selections as well.]

Knapp, Daniel, and Neil K. Snortum. *The Sounds of Chaucer's English: An Instructional Recording*. National Council of Teachers of English 868N–5778, 868N–5780, 868N–5782. [Side One has comments and drills on pronunciation; the other five sides contain selections from *Book of the Duchess, Parliament of Fowls, Troilus and Criseyde*, and *Canterbury Tales*. The reader allows time for the listener to repeat the ME lines, then again repeats the lines himself. Includes portions of the "General Prologue" and of the *Troilus and Criseyde* selections in the present textbook.]

Kökeritz, Helge. [See Pope and Kökeritz, *Beowulf and Chaucer*, above.]

INDEX